NTC's

FRENCH

GRAMMAR

Author
Isabelle Fournier

Consultant
Duncan Sidwell

National Textbook Company
a division of NTC/CONTEMPORARY PUBLISHING GROUP
Lincolnwood, Illinois USA

Library of Congress Cataloging-in-Publication Data

Fournier, Isabelle.
     NTC's French grammar / Isabelle Fournier.
         p.   cm.—(NTC's grammar series)
     Includes index.
     ISBN 0-8442-1493-0
     1. French language—Grammar—Handbooks, manuals, etc.
I. Title.   II. Series.
PC2112.F68   1997
448.2'421—dc21   97-38273
                                    CIP

Also available:
   NTC's Italian Grammar
   NTC's Spanish Grammar
   NTC's German Grammar

Cover artwork by Elaine Cox
Published in cooperation with BBC Enterprises Ltd.

This edition first published in 1998 by NTC Publishing Group
An imprint of NTC/Contemporary Publishing Company
4255 West Touhy Avenue
Lincolnwood (Chicago), Illinois 60646-1975 U.S.A.
Copyright © 1995, 1998 by Isabelle Fournier
Manufactured in the United States of America
International Standard Book Number: 0-8442-1493-0

15   14   13   12   11   10   9   8   7   6   5   4   3   2

■ Introduction

NTC's *French Grammar* is for adult learners whether learning at home or through adult education or nonspecialist continuing college language courses. It is also ideal for high school students.

It is a practical reference book that makes French grammar accessible to English-speaking learners, and it is the ideal complement to any course book. The emphasis is on clear and concise explanation of the core structures of French, illustrated by examples using current, everyday language.

It is not necessary to have a detailed formal knowledge of English grammar to use this book since the use of technical grammatical terms has been restricted to those that are essential. There is also a glossary to help clarify these terms.

The book is designed to allow easy and rapid consultation. It comprises:

- a list of contents—a quick way to find the section or subsection you want

- a glossary of grammatical terms

- grammar explanations clearly laid out in numbered sections and subsections. The first half of the book covers nouns, articles, adjectives, adverbs, pronouns, and prepositions. The second half focuses on verbs: formation, use, and irregular forms.

- verb tables—the patterns for regular verbs and for commonly used irregular verbs

- a comprehensive, easy-to-use index, which lists key words in French and English as well as grammatical terms

■ Contents

1 Glossary of Grammatical Terms   **9**

2 Accents   **18**
   2.1 Accents and Spelling Conventions

3 Punctuation and Capital Letters   **20**
   3.1 Punctuation   3.2 Capital Letters

4 Numbers   **24**
   4.1 Cardinal Numbers   4.2 Ordinal Numbers

5 Masculine and Feminine Nouns   **26**
   5.1 Nouns That Use Both Genders
   5.2 Nouns Referring to People

6 Plural of Nouns   **28**
   6.1 The Different Plural Forms 6.3 Proper Nouns
   6.2 Plural of Compound Nouns

7 *Le, la, l', les*   **30**
   7.1 Forms   7.2 Use

8 *Un, une, des*   **32**
   8.1 *Un, une*   8.2 *Des*

9 *Du, de la,* and *de l'*   **34**
   9.1 Forms   9.2 Use of *du, de la,* and *de l'*

10 The Use of *de*   **35**
   10.1 After a Negation   10.2 Before an Adjective

11 How Adjectives Show Gender and Number   **36**
   11.1 The Regular Pattern   11.2 Irregular Forms

12 Position of Adjectives   **39**

13 Adjectives Followed by a Preposition or a Conjunction   **40**
   13.1 Adjectives Followed by *de* 13.3 Adjective + *de* or *à* + infinitive
   13.2 Adjectives Followed by *à*   13.4 *Il est* + Adjective + *que...*

14 Formation of Adverbs   **42**
   14.1 Adverbs Ending in *-ment*   14.3 Alternatives to Adverbs
   14.2 Adverbs Not Ending in
         -ment

15 Position of Adverbs   **44**
   15.1 When Describing an   15.3 When Describing a Verb
         Adjective or Another Adverb   in a Compound Tense
   15.2 When Describing a Verb in a
         Simple Tense

16 Comparisons and Superlatives   **46**
16.1 The Comparative   16.2 The Superlative

17 Expressing Possession   **48**
17.1 The Use of *de*   17.3 Possessive Pronouns
17.2 Possessive Adjectives   17.4 *À moi*

18 Demonstratives   **51**
18.1 Demonstrative Adjectives   18.2 Demonstrative Pronouns

19 Indefinite Adjectives and Pronouns   **54**
19.1 Forms   19.2 Use

20 Questions and Exclamations   **57**
20.1 Asking a Direct Question   20.3 Indirect Questions
20.2 Asking *Who? What?*   20.4 Exclamations
      Which? etc.

21 Negatives   **61**
21.1 The Main Negatives   21.4 Leaving Out *pas*
21.2 Position of Negatives   21.5 Other Uses of *ne*
21.3 Leaving Out *ne*

22 Subject Pronouns   **65**
22.1 *Je*   22.3 *Il/Elle, Ils/Elles*
22.2 *Tu* and *Vous*   22.4 *On*

23 Object Pronouns   **67**
23.1 Forms   23.3 Word Order of Object
23.2 Direct or Indirect Pronoun?   Pronouns

24 *En*   **70**
24.1 Uses of *en*   24.2 Position of *en*

25 *Y*   **73**
25.1 Uses of *y*   25.2 Position of *y*

26 Reflexive and Emphatic Pronouns   **74**
26.1 Reflexive Pronouns   26.3 Use of *Soi*
26.2 Emphatic Pronouns

27 Relative Pronouns   **77**
27.1 Forms   27.4 Preposition Followed by a
27.2 *Qui* and *Que*   Relative Pronoun
27.3 *Ce qui, Ce que*   27.5 *Dont*
      27.6 *Où*

28 Prepositions   82
28.1 Using the Right Preposition   28.5 *Depuis, Pendant,* and *Il y a*
28.2 *À*   28.6 *Chez*
28.3 *En*   28.7 *Sur*
28.4 *De*

29 The Present Tense   92
29.1 Verbs Ending in *-er*   29.3 Irregular verbs
29.2 Verbs Ending in *-ir*   29.4 Use of the Present Tense

30 The *Passé Composé* Tense   98
30.1 The *Passé Composé* Tense Formed with *Avoir*
30.2 The *Passé Composé* Tense Formed with *Être*
30.3 The Agreement of Past Participles
30.4 Use of the *Passé Composé* Tense

31 The Imperfect Tense   102
31.1 Forms of the Imperfect   31.2 Use of the Imperfect Tense
Tense   31.3 Imperfect or *Passé Composé*?

32 The Pluperfect Tense   106
32.1 Forms of the Pluperfect   32.2 Use of the Pluperfect Tense
Tense

33 The *Passé Simple* Tense   107
33.1 Forms of the *Passé Simple* Tense
33.2 Use of the *Passé Simple* Tense

34 The Preterite Perfect Tense   109
34.1 Forms of the Preterite Perfect Tense
34.2 Use of the Preterite Perfect Tense

35 The Future Tense   110
35.1 Forms of the Future Tense
35.2 Use of the Future Tense
35.3 Other Ways to Express the Future

36 The Future Perfect Tense   113
36.1 Forms of the Future   36.2 Use of the Future
Perfect Tense   Perfect Tense

37 The Present Conditional Tense   114
37.1 Forms of the Present   37.2 Use of the Present
Conditional Tense   Conditional Tense

38 The Past Conditional Tense   117
38.1 Forms of the Past   38.2 Use of the Past Conditional
Conditional Tense   Tense

39 The Infinitive   118
39.1 Forms of the Infinitive   39.2 Use of the Infinitive

40 Participles   **120**
40.1 The Present Participle   40.2 The Past Participle

41 The Imperative   **125**
41.1 Forms   41.2 The Imperative with Object Pronouns

42 The Passive   **127**
42.1 Forming the Passive   42.2 Use of the Passive

43 The Subjunctive   **129**
43.1 Forms of the Present Subjunctive   43.3 Other Tenses of the Subjunctive
43.2 Use of the Present Subjunctive

44 Use of Modal Verbs and of *Être*   **136**
44.1 *Devoir*   44.4 *Savoir* and *Connaître*
44.2 *Vouloir*   44.5 *Falloir*
44.3 *Pouvoir*   44.6 "To be" is Not Always *Être*

45 Reflexive Verbs   **140**
45.1 Main Categories of Reflexive Verbs   45.2 Reflexive Pronouns Used for "each other"

46 Impersonal Verbs   **144**
46.1 Verbs Describing the Weather   46.4 *Il paraît que, il semble que, on dirait que*
46.2 How to Express "There is..."   46.5 *Il suffit*
46.3 *Il vaut mieux*   46.6 Reflexive Impersonal Forms
    46.7 A Question of Style

47 Verbs Used with Objects   **147**
47.1 Verbs and Direct Objects   47.3 Verbs That Take *de* + an Object
47.2 Verbs That Take *à* + an Object

48 Verbs Used with Infinitives   **151**
48.1 Verbs That Take an Infinitive Without a Preposition   48.3 Verbs That Take *de* + an Infinitive
48.2 Verbs That Take *à* + an Infinitive   48.4 Verbs That Take *par* + an Infinitive

49 Linking words   **156**
49.1 Coordinating Conjunctions   49.2 Subordinating Conjunctions

50 Word Order   **159**
50.1 Inversion   50.3 Other Differences Between French and English Word Order
50.2 No Change of Word Order

51 Conjugation of Regular Verbs   **162**
   51.1 Endings   51.2 Stems

52 Irregular Verbs   **164**

52.1	Aller	52.27	Ouvrir
52.2	S'asseoir	52.28	Paraître
52.3	Avoir	52.29	Partir
52.4	Battre	52.30	Peindre
52.5	Boire	52.31	Plaire
52.6	Conduire	52.32	Pleuvoir
52.7	Connaître	52.33	Pouvoir
52.8	Coudre	52.34	Prendre
52.9	Courir	52.35	Recevoir
52.10	Craindre	52.36	Résoudre
52.11	Croire	52.37	Rire
52.12	Cueillir	52.38	Savoir
52.13	Cuire	52.39	Sentir
52.14	Devoir	52.40	Servir
52.15	Dire	52.41	Sortir
52.16	Dormir	52.42	Suffire
52.17	Écrire	52.43	Suivre
52.18	Envoyer	52.44	Taire
52.19	Être	52.45	Tenir
52.20	Faire	52.46	Vaincre
52.21	Falloir	52.47	Valoir
52.22	Haïr	52.48	Venir
52.23	Lire	52.49	Vivre
52.24	Mettre	52.50	Voir
52.25	Mourir	52.51	Vouloir
52.26	Naître		

53 Index   **182**

Active
See Voice.

Adjective
An adjective is a word that describes a noun. For example:
*It is a **big** house.*
*The windows are **big**.*
*The garden is very **big**.*
*It is **bigger** than their old one.*

In English, the form of the adjective only changes for the comparative (*bigger*) and the superlative (*biggest*). In French, adjectives change to reflect the gender and number of the noun they describe.

Adverb
An adverb is a word that adds information about the verb, or about another adverb or adjective. For example:
*She read the text **carefully**.* [manner]
*Please wait **here**.* [place]
*The exam is **tomorrow**.* [time]
*The exam was **very** difficult.* [degree]
*Do you come here **often**?* [frequency]

Agreement
Agreement is when two or more words in a sentence must change together. For example, in English: *she walks—they walk*. Here, both the subject and the verb change to show singular or plural.

Article
In English, *a* and *an* are the **indefinite articles**, and *the* is the **definite article**. The definite article is used with a noun to refer to a particular example of something. For example:
*She has gone to **the** post office.*

The indefinite article is used with a noun to refer to something unknown or unspecified. For example:

*I need to go to **a** post office. Is there one nearby?*

Clause

A clause is a group of words. It usually includes a subject and a verb. For example:

The box is green. [one clause—one sentence]
If you have finished, | you can leave. [two clauses—one sentence]

Comparative

See **Adjective**.

Conditional

A conditional sentence contains a clause beginning with *if, unless,* etc., which states what must happen before the action of the other clause can be done. For example:

***If it rains,** we will have to go home.*
*You can't go to the university **unless you pass your exams.***

The conditional tense states what would happen.

*I **would** do it if you asked me.*

Conjunction

A conjunction is a word that makes a connection between words, phrases or clauses, such as *and, but, though, so, if, because.* For example:

*My present was small **but** nice.*
*The exam finished **so** we all went home.*

Definite Article

See **Article**.

Direct Object

See **Object**.

Feminine

See **Gender**.

Gender
Gender shows whether a word is masculine or feminine.
For example:
> *The **policeman** said that **he** saw the burglar.*
> [masculine noun and pronoun]
> *The **policewoman** said that **she** saw the burglar.*
> [feminine noun and pronoun]

In French, all nouns have a gender, even tables and
bicycles, e.g., *la table, le vélo*.

Imperative
See Mood.

Impersonal
Impersonal pronouns do not specify who or what does
something. For example:
> *It is raining.*
> *It's cold.*

Indefinite Article
See Article.

Indicative
See Mood.

Indirect Object
See Object.

Infinitive
The infinitive form of the verb is the base form, and the
form that usually appears in dictionaries. In English, the
infinitive is often used with *to* (e.g., *I'd like **to go***), but can
be used on its own (e.g., *I must **go**)*.

Interjection
An interjection is a word which shows an emotional state
or attitude. For example:
> ***Hey!*** *Come back here.*
> ***Oh!*** *That's terrible news.*

Interrogative

An interrogative sentence uses the form of a question. For example: *Did you open the window?*

Intransitive

See **Transitive**.

Masculine

See **Gender**.

Modal

Modal verbs are used with another verb to distinguish between possibility and actuality. For example:

*I **may** be late tonight.* [possibility]
*They **can** play outside.* [permission]

In English, the modal verbs are *can, could, have to, may, might, must, shall, should, will,* and *would.*

Mood

The mood of a verb can reveal a particular attitude to what is said or written, or toward the person being addressed. For example, in English you use the **indicative mood** to state or question what you consider to be facts:

*She **sat** down.*
Are** you **coming?

You use the **imperative mood** when you are telling or ordering someone to do something:

***Be** quiet!*
***Put** it on the table.*

You might use the **subjunctive mood** when you want to express wishes, possibilities, or doubts:

*It is essential that you **be** there.*
*If I **were** you, I'd do it.*

Negative

A word, phrase, or sentence that denies something is negative. In English, the most common way of showing this is with *not*. For example:

*I am **not** very happy!*

Noun

A noun refers to a person, a thing, or an abstract idea such as a feeling or quality. For example:

*The **woman** drove off.*
*The children patted the **dog**.*
*the dog's **bone***
*the big **boxes***
*Her **beauty** was world famous.*
*He's not afraid of **death**.*
*What a brilliant **idea**!*

Number

Number shows the difference between **singular** and **plural**. For example:

*The green **box is** empty.* [singular]
*The green **boxes are** empty.* [plural]

In English, nouns, pronouns, and verbs change to show number, but adjectives do not change. In French, adjectives change, too.

Object

Many verbs are used with objects. Objects are usually nouns or pronouns. The object is the noun or pronoun that is affected by the verb. The subject is the noun or pronoun that causes that effect. For example:

*I asked **a question**.* [direct object]
*I asked **him**.* [indirect object]
*I gave **him the keys**.* [indirect + direct object]

Participle

A participle is a form of the verb that can be used with other verbs, or sometimes as an adjective or a noun. For example:

*I like **walking** to work.* [present participle]

*We went on a **walking** holiday.*
***Walking** is good for you!*
*She has **broken** her arm.* [past participle]
*She has a **broken** arm.*

Passive

See **Voice**.

Person

Person is the system that shows the number of people talking or writing. For example:

I [first person singular]   *it* [third person singular]
you [second person singular]   *we* [first person plural]
he [third person singular]   *you* [second person plural]
she [third person singular]   *they* [third person plural]

In English, person is also shown in the verb form. For example:

*I **work** in Boston.* [first person verb]
*She **works** in Boston.* [third person verb]

See also **Pronoun** and **Possessive**.

Phrase

A phrase is a group of words that usually does not include a subject and a verb. For example:

***My favorite TV program** is Seinfeld.* [noun phrase]
*The window **had been open** all night.* [verb phrase]
*I didn't get home **until six o'clock**.* [prepositional phrase]
*His death was **very sad**.* [adjective phrase]
*We go out for a meal **every week**.* [adverb phrase]

Plural

Nouns, verbs, and pronouns that refer to more than one thing use a plural form. For example:

*The green **boxes** are empty.*
***They** are very tall.*

In French, adjectives also change to show singular and plural.

Possessive

A possessive is a word that shows ownership or possession. For example:

> *my, your, his, her, its, our, your, their* [possessive adjectives]
> *mine, yours, his, hers, ours, yours, theirs* [possessive pronouns]
> the **student's** books/the **students'** books [possessive nouns]

Preposition

A preposition is a word that is used before a noun or a pronoun, and that shows the relationship between that noun or pronoun and the rest of the sentence. For example:

> *I went **to** the library.*
> *I'll meet you **at** one o'clock.*

Pronoun

A pronoun is a word that is used instead of a noun or a noun phrase in a sentence. For example:

> *Where is Elspeth? **She** left the meeting early.*
> *Do you know **them**? I only know **him**.*

In English, the **personal pronouns** are:

> *I, you, he, she, it, we, you, they*

The **personal object pronouns** are:

> *me, you, him, her, it, us, you, them*

The **possessive pronouns** are:

> *mine, yours, his, hers, its, our, yours, theirs*

The **reflexive pronouns** are:

> *myself, yourself, himself, herself, itself, ourselves, yourselves, themselves*

Reflexive

A reflexive pronoun is used when the subject and the object of a sentence refer to the same person or thing. For example:

> *I hurt **myself**.*
> *The children are enjoying **themselves**.*

Sentence

A sentence is a group of words that (in written English) begins with a capital letter and ends with one of the punctuation marks [.?!]. For example:

The box is green.

Is the box green?

Put it in the green box!

Singular

Nouns, verbs, and pronouns that refer to only one thing use a singular form. For example:

*The green **box is** empty.*

***He is** very tall.*

In French, adjectives also change to show singular and plural.

Subject

The subject of a sentence is the word or phrase that represents the person or thing carrying out the action of the verb. For example:

***The student** is learning Italian.*

***The students** are learning Italian.*

In English, the subject is usually a noun or pronoun that comes before the main verb. See **Object**.

Subjunctive

See **Mood**.

Superlative

See **Adjective**.

Tense

The form of a verb shows whether you are referring to the past, the present, or the future. This system of forms is called the tense system. For example:

*The student **works** hard.* [present tense verb]

*The student **worked** hard.* [past tense verb]

Note that there is no simple relationship between tense and time. The English present tense can refer to present or future time. For example:

> I **live** in Boston. [present tense verb—present time]
>
> I **start** work tomorrow. [present tense verb—future time]

Transitive

A transitive verb is one which takes an object. For example: *They **saw** the film.*

An **intransitive** verb is one which does not take an object. For example: *We **danced** all night.* Note that many verbs can be used both transitively and intransitively:

> We **ate** and then went out.
>
> We **ate** a huge meal and then fell asleep.

Verb

A verb usually refers to an action or state. For example:

> The children **patted** the dog.
>
> The green box **is** empty.

The form of the verb can change to show tense, person, number, and mood.

Voice

The relationship between the verb and the noun phrases in a sentence can be made clear by using either the active or the passive voice. For example:

> The fire destroyed the house. [active voice]
>
> The house was destroyed by the fire. [passive voice]

Although the meaning of these two sentences is the same, in the active sentence *The fire* is the subject, while in the passive sentence *The house* is the subject. Voice is often used to change the emphasis of a sentence. It can also be used to avoid saying who did something.

2 Accents

Sections 2 and 3 look at how French uses accents, punctuation marks, and capital letters.

2.1 Accents and Spelling Conventions

In written French, the following accents are used:

´	l'accent aigu	acute accent
`	l'accent grave	grave accent
^	l'accent circonflexe	circumflex accent
¨	le tréma	diaeresis
ç	la cédille	cedilla

■ 2.1.1 The Acute Accent

The acute accent [´] is only used on an **e**. This is then pronounced like **et**. Compare: **je mange** (*I eat*) and **j'ai mangé** (*I ate*).

■ 2.1.2 The Grave Accent

The grave accent [`] is mainly used on an **e**. The sound **è** is more open than **é**. Compare: **j'achète** (*I buy*) and **j'ai acheté** (*I bought*).

The grave accent is also used on an **a** or **u** to distinguish two words that otherwise would look alike:

a (*has*)	Elle **a** rendez-vous à 4 heures. *She **has** an appointment at 4 o'clock.*
à (*at, to*)	Je vais **à** la banque. *I am going **to** the bank.*
la (*the*)	Elle est **la** P.D.G. de **la** société Piers. *She is **the** managing director of **the** Piers company.*
là (*here/ there*)	Elle n'est pas encore **là**. *She is not **here/there** yet.*

| **ou** (*or*) | Je pourrais venir mardi **ou** mercredi. *I could come on Tuesday or Wednesday.* |
| **où** (*where*) | Je ne sais pas **où** il est allé. *I don't know* **where** *he has gone.* |

■ 2.1.3 The Circumflex Accent

The circumflex accent [^] is used on **a, e, i, o,** and **u: être** (*to be*), **l'hôpital** (*hospital*), **les pâtes** (*pasta*). You may find it useful to know that these words used to have an **s** after the vowel—the **s** is often present in the English equivalent, for example, **un hôte** (*a host*).

ê sounds very much like **è**, while **â, î, ô,** and **û** sound nowadays very much the same as **a, i, o,** and **u**.

Note also the difference between **du** (*some*) and **dû** (past participle of **devoir**: *owed/due*):

J'ai **du** travail à faire. *I have **some** work to do.*
J'ai **dû** aller le chercher. *I **had to** pick him up.*

■ 2.1.4 The Diaeresis

The diaeresis [¨] is placed on a vowel to indicate that this vowel must be pronounced separately from the previous one: **Noël** (*Christmas*), **haïr** (*to hate*).

■ 2.1.5 The Cedilla

The cedilla is used with a **c** to obtain the sound [s] before **a, o,** or **u**:

Ça ne fait rien. *It doesn't matter.*
Nous **commençons** à 8 heures. *We start at 8 o'clock.*

Without a cedilla, **c** followed by **a, o,** or **u** is pronounced [k]: **couper** (*to cut*).

3 Punctuation and Capital Letters

3.1 Punctuation

French uses almost exactly the same punctuation marks as does English. The punctuation marks and other signs used in written French are as follows:

'	l'apostrophe (f.)	apostrophe
.	le point	full stop
,	la virgule	comma
;	le point-virgule	semicolon
:	le deux-points	colon
?	le point d'interrogation	question mark
!	le point d'exclamation	exclamation mark
-	le trait d'union	hyphen
—	le tiret	dash
...	les points de suspension	suspension points
( )	les parenthèses (f.)	parentheses
«...» or "..."	les guillemets (m.)	quotation marks

By and large, most punctuation marks are used in a similar way to English, with the exception of the apostrophe, the hyphen, the comma (with numbers), and quotation marks.

■ 3.1.1 Apostrophes

Apostrophes are used when a letter has been omitted, for ease of pronunciation. For example, when a noun or adjective starts with a vowel, l' is used instead of le or la:

Asseyez-vous à l'avant.   *Sit at the front.*

L' is used with most words that start with h: l'hôtel (*hotel*) and l'hiver (*winter*). The h is called a silent h because it is not sounded.

There are a few words beginning with **h** where **le** or **la** do not become **l'**: **le haricot** (*bean*), **le hasard** (*hazard/chance*), **la Hollande** (*Holland*). This **h** is called an aspirate **h**: although it is not spoken, it cannot be smoothed over like the **h** in **hôtel**, and in the plural no liaison is possible when preceded by **les/des** or a plural adjective. For example, no liaison should be made between **les** and **haricots** or **Hollandais**.

Similarly, **de**, **ne**, **que**, and the personal pronouns **je**, **me**, and **te** lose their **-e** before a vowel or a silent **h**:

C'est la voiture **d'**une amie.	*It is a friend's car.*
Ce **n'**est pas la peine.	*It is not worth it.*
Je crois **qu'**il va mieux.	*I think that he is better.*
J'arriverai vers dix heures.	*I'll arive at about ten o'clock.*
Il **t'**a vu.	*He saw you.*

Note also that:

- **ça/ce** becomes **c'** before **est** but not before other vowels:
C'est une chance!	*It's lucky!*
Ça arrive!	*It happens!*

- **si** becomes **s'**, but only when followed by **il** or **ils** (not **elle** or **elles**):
Je ne sais pas **s'**ils viendront/	*I don't know if they will*
si elles viendront.	*come.*

■ 3.1.2 The Hyphen
The hyphen is used:

- when a word is made up of two or more elements: **un porte-clefs** (*a key ring*), **celui-ci** (*this one*), **c'est-à-dire** (*that is to say*)

- for compound numbers between 17 and 99 when they are not linked by **et**: compare **vingt et un** and **vingt-deux**

- in inversions, to link the verb and the subject pronoun:
  Avez-vous de la monnaie?   *Do you have any change?*

■ 3.1.3 The Comma
The use of commas is similar to English, except in figures:

- The comma is used for decimals: **2,5%** (read as: **deux virgule cinq pour cent**);

- but not for thousands or larger numbers. A space or a full stop is used instead: **2 500** or **2.500**.

■ 3.1.4 Quotation Marks
Note that:

- the most commonly used quotation marks are «...»

- the person speaking can be referred to without having to close and reopen quotation marks:

  "C'est un contrat exceptionnel, a déclaré le porte-parole. Il permettra de créer une centaine d'emplois."   *"It's an exceptional contract," said the spokesman. "It will generate about a hundred new jobs."*

- a dash is widely used for conversations:

  —Passez une bonne soirée! me dit-il chaleureusement.
  —Merci bien. De même! répondis-je en souriant.
  "Have a nice evening!" he said warmly. "Thank you. The same to you!" I answered with a smile.

3.2 Capital Letters
Capital letters are used for the first word of a sentence and for names of people or places. However:

- names of days or months are normally written in small letters:

  J'arriverai lundi, le 5 **septembre**.   *I'll arrive on Monday, September 5.*

- for nationalities, capital letters are used only for nouns, not for adjectives. Compare these examples:
  Elle est **française**.   *She is French.*
  J'ai rencontré une **Française**.   *I have met a Frenchwoman.*

- names of languages do not take capital letters:
  J'apprends le **russe**.   *I am learning Russian.*

- names of products that derive from the name of a place do not take a capital letter: **le bordeaux** (*Claret*), **le brie** (*Brie cheese*)

4 Numbers

4.1 Cardinal Numbers

1	un, une	51	cinquante et un
2	deux	52	cinquante-deux
3	trois	60	soixante
4	quatre	61	soixante et un
5	cinq	62	soixante-deux
6	six	70	soixante-dix
7	sept	71	soixante et onze
8	huit	72	soixante-douze
9	neuf	73	soixante-treize
10	dix	74	soixante-quatorze
11	onze	75	soixante-quinze
12	douze	76	soixante-seize
13	treize	77	soixante-dix-sept
14	quatorze	78	soixante-dix-huit
15	quinze	79	soixante-dix-neuf
16	seize	80	quatre-vingts
17	dix-sept	81	quatre-vingt-un
18	dix-huit	82	quatre-vingt-deux
19	dix-neuf	90	quatre-vingt-dix
20	vingt	91	quatre-vingt-onze
21	vingt et un	100	cent
22	vingt-deux	101	cent un, etc.
30	trente	200	deux cents
31	trente et un	201	deux cent un
32	trente-deux	1 000	mille
40	quarante	2 000	deux mille
41	quarante et un	2001	deux mille un
42	quarante-deux	100 000	cent mille
50	cinquante	1 000 000	un million

In some French-speaking countries (e.g., Canada, Belgium, Switzerland), different numbers are used: **septante** (*70*), **octante** (*80*), and **nonante** (*90*).

Numbers used on their own are masculine. The article **le**
(not **l'**) is used, even before **huit** and **onze**:

Le 21 est le numéro gagnant.   *The winning number is 21.*
Le huit et le onze.   *Eight and eleven.*

Un is the only cardinal number that agrees with a noun
in gender: **un kilo** (*one kilo*), **une livre** (*one pound*).

Cent takes an **-s** when preceded by another number as
long as it is not followed by another number: **trois cents**
but **trois cent vingt**. **Vingt**, when it appears in **quatre-
vingts**, also takes an **-s** when it is not followed by
another number: **quatre-vingts** but **quatre-vingt-un**.

Cent and **mille** cannot be preceded by **un**, and **mille**
never takes an **s**.

To show that a number is only approximate, you can add
the ending **aine** to **douze**, **quinze**, **cent**, and decimal
numbers: **une quinzaine** (*about fifteen*), **une trentaine**
(*about thirty*).

4.2 Ordinal Numbers

Most ordinal numbers are formed by adding **-ième** to the
cardinal numbers: **deuxième** (*2nd*), **troisième** (*3rd*), etc.
(Numbers ending in **-e** lose that **-e** as ordinal numbers:
quatre, **quatrième**.) Exceptions are: **premier** (*1st*), **second**
(*2nd*), **cinquième** (*5th*), **neuvième** (*9th*).

Ordinal numbers agree with the noun they refer to in
gender and number: **le premier jour** (*the first day*), **la
première semaine** (*the first week*).

Ordinal numbers are used for dates and for names of
monarchs only for *first*; cardinal numbers are used
otherwise: **le premier et le deux mars** (*the first and the
second of March*), **Napoléon 1er** (read as: *premier*),
Napoléon III (read as: *trois*).

5 Masculine and Feminine Nouns

Nouns are words that represent things, people, or ideas, for example **maison**, **garçon**, **générosité** (*house*, *boy*, *generosity*) are nouns.

In French, nearly all nouns are masculine or feminine. This is indicated in dictionaries or word lists by an (**m**) or (**nm**) next to a masculine noun and an (**f**) or (**nf**) next to a feminine noun. The gender of most nouns is just a convention and needs to be learned or checked in a dictionary.

Most feminine nouns end in -**e** while most masculine nouns end with a consonant. Compare: **un an** (*a year*) and **une année** (*a year*).

A large number of masculine nouns do end, however, in -**e**: **le groupe** (*group*), **le monde** (*world*), **le silence** (*silence*).

5.1 Nouns That Use Both Genders

Beware that a few nouns have different meanings depending on their gender. Here are some of the most common ones:

un livre *book*	une livre *pound*
le poste *TV/radio set*	la poste *post office*
le tour *turn, round*	la tour *tower*

5.2 Nouns Referring to People

■ 5.2.1 A few nouns designating people use the same form for males and females. They are indicated in dictionaries and wordlists by (**m/f**) or (**nmf**). Most of them can be used with a masculine or a feminine article as appropriate. For example:

un/une dentiste	*a dentist*
un/une élève	*a pupil*
un/une enfant	*a child*

A few names of professions, however, can only be used with a masculine article, even when referring to a woman:

un docteur/médecin   *a doctor*
un ingénieur   *an engineer*
un professeur   *a teacher*

■ **5.2.2** Most nouns designating people and animals have, however, a masculine and a feminine form. Most add an -e for the feminine form: **un marchand/une marchande** (*a shopkeeper*). But many undergo a more drastic change. Note the following patterns:

-er/-ère	un boulanger/une boulangère	*a baker*
-en/-enne -an/-anne -on/-onne	un Italien/une Italienne un paysan/une paysanne un lion/une lionne	*an Italian* *a farmer* *a lion/lioness*
-at/-atte	un chat/une chatte	*a cat*
-eur /-euse -eur/-rice	un vendeur/une vendeuse un acteur/une actrice	*a sales assistant* *an actor/ actress*
-f/-ve	un veuf/une veuve	*a widower/ widow*
-x /-se	un époux/une épouse	*a spouse*

■ **5.2.3** Some nouns are feminine, even when they refer to a man:

une connaissance   *an acquaintance*
une personne   *a person*
une victime   *a victim*

6 Plural of Nouns

When a noun refers to more than one person or thing it takes the plural form. This may simply mean adding an -s to the end of the noun, or it may involve other changes (or occasionally no change at all).

6.1 The Different Plural Forms

Most nouns add -s in the plural: **le produit** (*the product*), **les produits** (*the products*). In spoken French the -s is not pronounced. If a noun already ends in -s, -x, or -z it does not change in the plural:

le fils *the son*	les fils *the sons*
le prix *the price*	les prix *the prices*
le nez *the nose*	les nez *the noses*

A number of nouns take an -x or -ux in the plural. Among them are:

- most nouns ending in -al, -eu, -au, or -eau:

le journal *the newspaper*	les journaux *the newspapers*
un cheveu *a hair*	des cheveux *hair, hairs*
le château *the castle*	les châteaux *the castles*

- a few nouns ending in -ou and -ail:

bijou *the jewel*	les bijoux *the jewels*
le chou *the cabbage*	les choux *the cabbages*
le genou *the knee*	les genoux *the knees*
le travail *work*	les travaux *the works*

Note also the following irregular plurals:

Madame *Madam/Mrs/Ms*	Mesdames *Ladies*
Mademoiselle *Miss*	Mesdemoiselles *Misses*
Monsieur *Mr/gentleman*	Messieurs *gentlemen*
l'œil *the eye*	les yeux *the eyes*
le ciel *the sky*	les cieux *the skies*

6.2 Plural of Compound Nouns

Nouns made up of two components generally add an -s
(or -x) to any part which is an adjective or a plural noun:
les grands-parents (*grandparents*).

The -s or -x is not added to a component which is a verb
form, a preposition, or a singular noun:

des porte-clés	*key rings*
des porte-monnaie	*purses*
des arrière-grands-parents	*great-grandparents*

6.3 Proper Nouns

Family names are invariable, except for historical names:

Tu as vu les Dupont récemment?	*Have you seen the Duponts recently?*
Il a écrit un livre sur les Bourbons.	*He has written a book about the Bourbons.*

7 Le, la, l', les

Le, **la**, **l'**, and **les** are definite articles. They correspond to the English article *the*, though there are a number of cases where they are used in French but not in English.

7.1 Forms

There are four forms: **le**, **la**, **l'**, and **les**. The form of the definite article varies according to the word it precedes:

before a masculine noun	le	**le** père *the father* **le** jardin *the garden*
before a feminine noun	la	**la** mère *the mother* **la** maison *the house*
before a singular word starting with a vowel or a silent **h**	l'	**l'**eau (f.) *the water* **l'**hôtel (m.) *the hotel*
before a plural noun	les	**les** enfants *the children*

When **le** and **les** are used with **de** or **à**, they change as follows:

de + le = du **de + les = des**	**à + le = au** **à + les = aux**

Je viens **du** bureau.   *I have just come from the office.*
Nous allons **au** cinéma.   *We are going to the movies.*

7.2 Use

Le, **la**, **l'**, and **les** are used when in English the article *the* is used:

Vous avez visité **la** maison   *Have you looked at the house*
qui est à vendre rue   *which is for sale in the rue*
Camus?   *Camus?*

They are also used in a number of cases where *the* is not used in English:

- when referring to a category of people, animals, or things:

  Il aime **les** bonbons.   *He likes candy.*

- with abstract nouns:

  Le chômage, **la** drogue, et **la** délinquance sont devenus des problèmes quotidiens.   *Unemployment, drug addiction, and delinquency have become common problems.*

- with names of days, parts of days, and seasons, to express regularity: *le* **lundi** (*on Mondays*), *l'***hiver** (*in winter*)

- with geographical names: *la* **France**, *l'***Australie** (except after **en, au,** or **aux:** *en Angleterre,* see 28.1.1)

- with names of languages, school subjects, and sports:

  J'ai appris **l'**espagnol à **l'**école.   *I learned Spanish at school.*
  L'équitation est son sport préféré.   *Horseback riding is her favorite sport.*

- in expressions of price or speed: **15 francs *le* kilo** (*15 francs a kilo [2.2 pounds]*), **90 km à *l'*heure** (*90 kilometers [56 miles] per hour*);

- when giving a number:

  Mon numéro de téléphone est **le** 57 54 00 14.   *My phone number is 57 54 00 14.*

- with parts of the body:

  Il a **les** yeux bleus.   *He has blue eyes.*
  Je me lave **les** mains.   *I wash my hands.* (See 17.2.)

- with titles: *la* **Princesse Stéphanie** (*Princess Stephanie*), **Monsieur *le* Président** (*the /Mr. President*).

8 Un, une, des

Un, **une**, and **des** are indefinite articles. They correspond to the English articles *a*, *some*, and *any*.

8.1 Un, une

Un and **une** are equivalent to the English article *a*.
Use **un** before a masculine noun: **un jardin** (*a garden*).
Use **une** before a feminine noun: **une maison** (*a house*).

Il portait **un** costume clair et **une** chemise noire.	*He was wearing a light suit and a black shirt.*

You cannot use **un** or **une**:

- when stating someone's occupation, nationality, or religion:

Elle est médecin.	*She is a doctor.*
Il travaille comme comptable.	*He works as an accountant.*

  Except after **c'est**:

C'est **un** bon médecin.	*He/she is a good doctor.*

- before **cent** (*a hundred*) and **mille** (*a thousand*):

Je lui ai donné cent francs.	*I gave him a hundred francs.*

- after most negations (see 21.1):

Nous n'avons pas de jardin.	*We don't have a garden.*

8.2 Des

The article **des** is used before plural nouns. It refers to an unspecified group of things, people, or animals, while **les** refers to a specific group of things, people, or animals. Compare:

Tu as vu **des** enfants?	*Did you see **any** children?*
Tu as vu **les** enfants?	*Did you see **the** children?*

Note that **des** cannot be left out as it often is in English.

So **Vous avez des timbres?** can mean: *Do you have **stamps?***
*Do you have **some stamps?*** or *Do you have **any stamps?***

Like **un** and **une, des** cannot be used:

- when stating people's occupation, nationality, or religion, except after **ce sont:**

Ils sont informaticiens.	*They are computer scientists.*
Ce sont **des** comptables.	*They are accountants.*

- nor after most negations (see 10.1):

Il n'ont pas d'enfants.	*They don't have any children.*

Note that **des** is usually replaced by **de** before an adjective that precedes a plural noun (see 10.2). It cannot be used after an expression of quantity:

Ils ont beaucoup **de** jeux vidéos.	*They have lots of computer games.*

9   *Du, de la,* and *de l'*

Du, de la, and **de l'** are used to indicate an indeterminate quantity: **Vous voulez** *du* **café?** (*Would you like some coffee?*) **Vous avez** *de la* **confiture?** (*Do you have any jam?*).

9.1 Forms

The forms are as follows:

before a masculine noun	**du**	Je voudrais **du** café. *I'd like some coffee.*
before a feminine noun	**de la**	Je voudrais **de la** bière. *I'd like some beer.*
before a word starting with a vowel or a silent **h**	**de l'**	Je voudrais **de l'**eau. *I'd like some water.*

9.2 Use of *du, de la,* and *de l'*

Du, de la, and **de l'** are used when referring to an indeterminate quantity. Compare these two examples:

| Je voudrais **du** pain, s'il vous plaît. | *I'd like **some** bread, please.* |
| Je voudrais **un** pain, s'il vous plaît. | *I'd like **a** loaf of bread, please.* |

Du, de la, and **de l'** cannot be left out in the way that *some* and *any* often are in English:

| Vous voulez **du** sucre? | *Would you like sugar?/Would you like any sugar?* |

In some cases, **de** is used instead of **du, de la,** and **de l'** (see 10).

10 The Use of *de*

In some cases, **de** (or **d'**) is used instead of **un, une, des, du, de la, de l'**. (See also 28.4.)

10.1 After a Negation

De or **d'** is used (instead of **un, une, des, du, de la**, or **de l'**) after all negations except *ne... que* (see 21):

Je n'ai plus **de** sucre.	*I don't have any sugar left.*
Je n'ai acheté que **du** pain.	*I only bought bread.*

Un, une, and **des** are still used after **ce n'est pas** and **ce ne sont pas**.

Ce n'est pas **un** vin sec, c'est un vin doux.	*It is not a dry wine, it is a sweet wine.*

10.2 Before an Adjective

De is used instead of **des** when an adjective precedes a plural noun:

Nous avons visité **de** très beaux châteaux.	*We visited some very beautiful castles.*

This does not happen when the adjective and the noun form a set expression:

Des petites filles jouaient dans la rue.	*Some girls were playing in the street.*
Vous reprenez **des** petits pois?	*Would you like some more peas?*

11 How Adjectives Show Gender and Number

Adjectives are words like **petit** (*small*) or **intéressant** (*interesting*). They describe nouns—**le jardin est petit** (*the garden is small*) or pronouns—**il est petit** (*it is small*). Adjectives agree with the noun or pronoun they refer to. The masculine singular form is the one given first in a dictionary or word list (**petit**, *little*).

11.1 The Regular Pattern

Most adjectives add:

-e	when describing a feminine noun or pronoun:
	C'est une **grande** maison. *It is a big house.*
	Elle est **grande**. *She/It is big.*
-es	when describing a feminine plural noun or pronoun:
	Les fenêtres sont **grandes**. *The windows are big.*
-s	when describing a masculine plural noun or pronoun:
	Il y a de **grands** fauteuils. *There are big armchairs.*
	or several nouns of different genders:
	La cour et le jardin sont **grands**. *The courtyard and the garden are big.*

Most adjectives ending in **-eau** or **-al** add an **-x** when describing a masculine plural noun (see 6.1):

Il y a de **beaux** dessins.   *There are beautiful drawings.*

Note that:

• the effect of adding an **-e** to the end of an adjective is to have a final consonant sounded, not silent: in **grande maison** the **d** is pronounced, but not in **grand jardin**

- adjectives that already end in **-e** in the masculine do not change in the feminine:

un jeune homme	*a young man*
une jeune femme	*a young woman*

- when the adjective ends in **-s** or **-x** no extra **s** is added:

un gros nuage	*a big cloud*
de gros nuages	*big clouds*

- when the adjective describes the pronouns **on** or **vous**, it is common to make it agree with the gender and number of the person(s) in mind:

On est ravi**s**.	***We** are delighted.*

A very small number of adjectives do not change in the feminine or plural. This happens with:

- colors that get their name from fruit:

Il a les yeux marron.	*He has brown eyes.*
(marron = *chestnut*)	

- colors in compound forms:

Vous avez des pulls bleu marine?	*Do you have any navy blue pullovers?*

11.2 Irregular Forms

Most irregular forms of adjectives occur in the feminine. A few adjectives have, however, an irregular masculine form when used before a noun starting with a vowel or a silent **h** (these forms are marked with an asterisk in the list below). Here are the most common irregular forms:

	Masculine	Feminine	
-nne	bon mignon ancien	bonne mignonne ancienne	*good* *good-looking, sweet* *ancient, former*

	Masculine	**Feminine**	
-lle	beau/bel*	belle	*beautiful*
	nouveau/nouvel*	nouvelle	*new*
	nul	nulle	*nil, useless*
	vieux/vieil*	vieille	*old*
	gentil	gentille	*kind*
-ère	cher	chère	*dear*
-ète	complet	complète	*complete*
-ette	net	nette	*clear*
-euse	menteur	menteuse	*false, lying*
-rice	séducteur	séductrice	*seductive*
-ve	neuf	neuve	*new*
-se	heureux	heureuse	*happy*
-che	blanc	blanche	*white*
	frais	fraîche	*fresh*
-que	public	publique	*public*
-gue	long	longue	*long*
-uë	ambigu	ambiguë	*ambiguous*

C'est une vieille église.   *It's an old church.*
C'est un vieil ami.   *He's an old friend.*
Tu as pris ce vieux vélo?   *You took that old bike?*

*Irregular masculine form before a vowel or silent **h**

12 Position of Adjectives

Adjectives normally come after the noun. In particular, adjectives of color, shape, and nationality always do:

C'est une voiture japonaise.   *It's a Japanese car.*

However, cardinal numbers—**premier** (*first*), **deuxième** (*second*), etc.—usually come before the noun, as do the following adjectives: **beau** (*beautiful*), **bon** (*good*), **court** (*short*), **dernier** (*last*), **gentil** (*kind*), **grand** (*big, tall*), **gros** (*big, fat*), **haut** (*tall*), **jeune** (*young*), **joli** (*pretty*), **long** (*long*), **mauvais** (*bad*), **nouveau** (*new*), **petit** (*little*), **vieux** (*old*).

C'est un bon restaurant.   *It's a good restaurant.*

When several adjectives describe one noun, the rules above still apply:

Il y a un bon restaurant italien.   *There is a good Italian restaurant.*

In a very few cases, the adjective means something different according to whether it is placed before or after the noun. For example:

	Before the noun	After the noun
ancien	*former*	*old, ancient*
même	*same*	*very*
propre	*own*	*clean*
seul	*single*	*on one's own*
simple	*mere*	*easy*

C'est une voiture propre.   *It is a clean car.*
C'est ma propre voiture.   *It is my own car.*

13 Adjectives Followed by a Preposition or a Conjunction

Some adjectives can be followed by a noun, a pronoun, or an infinitive. A preposition is then needed to link the adjective and the other word. Some adjectives can also be followed by **que** and the subjunctive.

13.1 Adjectives Followed by *de*

Adjectives expressing a feeling (e.g., **heureux**, *happy*; **content**, *happy*; **enchanté**, *delighted*; **ravi**, *delighted*; **malheureux**, *unhappy*; **triste**, *sad*; **désolé**, *sorry*; **fâché**, *angry*; **fier**, *proud*; etc.) take **de** when followed by a noun, a pronoun, or an infinitive:

Je suis content **de** lui.	*I am pleased with him.*
Heureux **de** faire votre connaissance.	*Pleased to meet you.*

Adjectives expressing an ability (e.g., **capable**, *capable*) or a certitude (e.g., **certain**, *certain*; **sûr**, *sure*) can be followed by **de** and a noun, a pronoun, or an infinitive:

Je suis capable **de** le faire moi-même.	*I am capable of doing it myself.*
Vous êtes certain **des** résultats?	*Are you certain of the results?*

13.2 Adjectives Followed by *à*

Cardinal numbers (**premier**, *first*; **deuxième**, *second*; etc.) and a few adjectives take **à** when followed by a noun, a pronoun, or an infinitive. Here are the most common ones:

lent à	*slow to*	seul à	*the only one to*
prêt à	*ready to*	dernier à	*last to*
Je suis prête à partir.	*I am ready to go.*		

13.3 Adjective + *de* or *à* + Infinitive

Many adjectives of degree—such as **facile** (*easy*), **difficile**

(*difficult*), **possible** (*possible*), **impossible** (*impossible*),
intéressant (*interesting*), and **agréable** (*pleasant*)—can be
followed by either **de** or **à**. As a rule, use **de** when making
a general statement and **à** when talking about something
or someone specific. Compare the following examples:

when referring to something specific	C'est facile **à** faire. *It's easy to do.* (*Ce* refers to something that has just been mentioned.)
when referring to someone specific	Il est facile **à** comprendre. *He is easy to understand.*
when making a general statement	Il est facile **de** se tromper. *It's easy to make a mistake.* (*Il* doesn't refer to anything in particular.)

Adjectives expressing a necessity like **important** (*important*),
nécessaire (*necessary*), **indispensable** (*essential*), etc. are
normally used with **de**:

Il est important **de** réagir vite. *It is important to react quickly.*

13.4 *Il est* + Adjective + *que...*

The subjunctive is sometimes needed after the construction
il est + adjective + **que**, depending on the meaning of the
adjective (see 43.2).

Il est possible qu'il soit trop tard.   *It may be too late.*

14 Formation of Adverbs

Adverbs are words like **lentement** (*slowly*) or **bien** (*well*). They complete or add to the meaning of a verb, an adjective, or even another adverb:

Il travaille **bien**.	*He works well.*
Ce jardin est **très** joli!	*This garden is very beautiful!*
Elle le fait **très bien**.	*She does it very well.*

14.1 Adverbs Ending in *-ment*

In French many adverbs of manner end in **-ment**, for example **régulièrement** (*regularly*).

This **-ment** ending is usually added to the feminine form of the adjective:

Adjective	Adverb
malheureux/malheureuse *unhappy* nouveau/nouvelle *new*	malheureusement *unfortunately* nouvellement *newly*

Exceptions are: **absolument** (*absolutely*), **vraiment** (*truly*), **brièvement** (*briefly*), and **gentiment** (*kindly*).

Most adverbs derived from adjectives ending in -**ent** or -**ant** end in -**emment** or -**amment**:

Adjective	Adverb
prudent *careful* constant *constant*	prudemment *carefully* constamment *constantly*

Evidemment, je ne lui ai rien dit.	*Of course, I didn't tell him anything.*

Lentement (*slowly*) is an exception.

A few adverbs end in **-ément**. For example:

énormément	*enormously*
intensément	*intensively*
précisément	*precisely*
profondément	*deeply*

14.2 Adverbs Not Ending in *-ment*

A few adverbs of manner do not have a **-ment** ending:

Adjective	Adverb
bon *good*	bien *well*
mauvais *bad*	mal *badly*
meilleur *better*	mieux *better*

Adverbs that are not derived from adjectives—most adverbs of position, place, quantity, and time—do not end in **-ment**. For example:

Vous allez **loin**?	*Are you going far?*
J'en ai **assez**.	*I have had enough.*
Il viendra **bientôt**.	*He'll soon come.*

In a few set expressions, adjectives are used as adverbs, and so are invariable:

Elle a travaillé **dur**.	*She worked hard.*

14.3 Alternatives to Adverbs

A French speaker may describe an action or state by using a preposition and a noun, or an adverbial phrase, where in English an adverb is used:

Il a accepté notre invitation **avec enthousiasme**.	*He enthusiastically accepted our invitation.*
Il faut intervenir **d'urgence**.	*We must intervene urgently.*

15 Position of Adverbs

The position of French adverbs can be quite different from that of English adverbs. Here are some general rules.

15.1 When Describing an Adjective or Another Adverb

When an adverb is used to complete the meaning of an adjective or another adverb, it comes just before the word it describes:

Vous êtes **trop** aimable!	*You are too kind!*
Ils ont **très** bien travaillé.	*They worked very well.*

Très cannot be used before **beaucoup**, so do not translate *very much* literally.

15.2 When Describing a Verb in a Simple Tense

When the verb is in a simple tense (i.e., in the present, imperfect, future, and present conditional tenses), adverbs usually come after the verb they describe:

Il dit **toujours** ça.	*He always says that.*
Je n'aime pas **tellement** cette couleur.	*I don't like this color very much.*

15.3 When Describing a Verb in a Compound Tense

In compound tenses (i.e., in the **passé composé** and the pluperfect tenses, etc.), some adverbs come between the auxiliary (the **avoir** or **être** form) and the past participle, and some come after the past participle:

J'y suis **souvent** allée.	*I have often been there.*
J'y suis allée **régulièrement**.	*I went there regularly.*

■ 15.3.1 The following adverbs come *before* the past participle:

* adverbs of quantity:
  J'ai **trop** mangé.   *I have eaten too much.*
  Cela m'a **beaucoup** plu.   *I liked that very much.*

* some adverbs of time (**bientôt**, *soon*; **déjà**, *already*;
  encore, *yet*; **enfin**, *finally*; **rarement**, *rarely*; **souvent**,
  often; and **toujours**, *always*):
  Elle a **déjà** fini.   *She has already finished.*
  Je ne l'ai pas **encore** fait.   *I haven't done it yet.*

* a few adverbs of manner (**bien**, *well*; **mal**, *badly*; **mieux**,
  better; **vraiment**, *truly*; and **malheureusement**,
  unfortunately are the most common ones):
  Il a très **bien** travaillé.   *He has worked very well.*

■ 15.3.2 The following adverbs come *after* the past
participle:

* most adverbs of manner:
  Il a parlé très **vite**.   *He spoke very fast.*
  Elle a conduit **prudemment**.   *She drove carefully.*

* adverbs of place:
  Je l'ai cherché **partout**.   *I have looked for it everywhere.*

* adverbs of time—except for the ones mentioned above
  —for example **tôt** (*early*), **tard** (*late*), **aujourd'hui**
  (*today*), **demain** (*tomorrow*), **hier** (*yesterday*), and
  quelquefois (*sometimes*):
  Ils sont arrivés **tard** hier soir. *They arrived late last night.*

16 Comparisons and Superlatives

When comparing two people or things a comparative is used. When saying that someone or something is the best, the biggest, etc., a superlative is used.

16.1 The Comparative

You can make comparisons using:

plus... (que)	*more . . . (than)*
moins... (que)	*less . . . (than)*
aussi... (que)	*as . . . (as)*
autant... (que)	*as much . . . (as)*
davantage... (que)	*more . . . (than)*
Elle est **plus** grande **que** moi.	*She is taller than I am.*

A few adjectives and adverbs have irregular comparative forms:

- The comparative of **bon** (*good*) is **meilleur** (*better*) and of **bien** (*well*) is **mieux** (*better*):

  Ce vin est **bon** mais l'autre est **meilleur**.
  This wine is good, but the other one is better.

  Je vais beaucoup **mieux**.
  I am a lot better.

- **Pire** (*worse*) is used instead of **plus mauvais** or **plus mal** when making a judgement on someone's behavior or a situation:

  Il a perdu son emploi, ce qui est encore **pire**.
  He has lost his job, which is even worse.

- **Moindre** (*the smallest, the least*) is often used instead of **plus petit** when referring to something which is not measurable:

  Il n'a pas le **moindre** accent.
  He doesn't have the slightest accent.

While comparatives are often used with adjectives, they are also used with nouns. **Davantage** (*more*) can only be used this way.

Note that **de** is used instead of **que**:

- to link **plus**, **davantage**, **moins**, and **autant** with a noun:
  Il y a davantage **de** choix.   *There is more choice.*

- when **plus** and **moins** are used with a figure:
  La chambre coûte plus   *The room costs more than*
  de 200 Francs.   *200 Francs.*

16.2 The Superlative

To express that someone or something is *the biggest*, *the most*, or *the least*, you simply use **le, la,** or **les** in front of **plus** or **moins**:
  C'est **la** plus belle plage.   *It is the nicest beach.*

The article **le, la,** or **les** is repeated when the adjective follows the noun:
  C'est l'hôtel **le** plus   *It's the most comfortable hotel.*
  confortable.

To express *in* after a superlative, use **de**:
  C'est le meilleur hôtel   *It's the best hotel **in** town.*
  de la ville.

Note the construction superlative + **que** + subjunctive (see 43.2.3):
  C'est la plus belle ville   *It's the most beautiful town*
  que je connaisse.   *that I know.*

17 Expressing Possession

There are four different ways of expressing possession in French. For example:

C'est le sac **de** Mme Malraux.	*It is Mrs. Malraux's bag.*
C'est **son** sac.	*It is her bag.*
C'est **le sien**.	*It is hers.*
Il est **à elle**.	*It is hers.*

17.1 The Use of *de*

When talking about someone's relatives, acquaintances, or possessions, **de** is used to link the two nouns. Note how different the French construction is from the English one:

les enfants **de** mon frère	*my brother's children*
la voiture **de** Paul	*Paul's car*
les amis **d'**Anna	*Anna's friends*

De plus the definite article is also used to link two items, or a person to something inanimate:

la clé **de** la voiture	*the car key*
le maire **de** la ville	*the town's mayor*

Du is used instead of **de** + **le**, and **des** instead of **de** + **les**:

le directeur **du** collège	*the school's principal*
les jouets **des** enfants	*the children's toys*

17.2 Possessive Adjectives

Possessive adjectives—words like **mon, ma, mes** (*my*)— agree in gender and number with the noun that follows. They do not agree with the possessor: **son frère** can mean *his brother* or *her brother*.

Emilie m'a présenté à **son** père,	*Emilie has introduced me to*
mais pas encore à **sa** mère.	*her father, but not yet to her*
	mother.

Mon, ton, and **son** are, however, used in front of a feminine noun if it begins with a vowel or a silent **h**.

These are the possessive adjectives when only one person possesses something or someone:

	my	*your* (tu)	*his/her/its/one's*
masculine noun or one starting with a vowel or an **h**	**mon** mon père mon amie	**ton** ton jardin ton appartement	**son** son père son hôtel
feminine noun	**ma** ma maison	**ta** ta voiture	**sa** sa mère
plural noun (masculine or feminine)	**mes** mes amies	**tes** tes livres	**ses** ses lunettes

These are the possessive adjectives when more than one person possesses something or someone:

	our	*your* (vous)	*their*
singular noun (masculine or feminine)	**notre** notre père	**votre** votre maison	**leur** leur hôtel
plural noun (masculine or feminine)	**nos** nos enfants	**vos** vos cousines	**leurs** leurs amis

Possessive adjectives are not used before parts of the body when the person they belong to is mentioned in the same sentence:

Je me suis coupé **le doigt**. *I have cut my finger.*
Elle a levé **les yeux**. *She raised her eyes.*

17.3 Possessive Pronouns

Possessive pronouns are words like **le mien** (*mine*). They agree with the noun they stand for. They are as follows when one person is the possessor:

	mine	*yours* (**tu**)	*his/hers/its*
masculine singular	**le mien**	**le tien**	**le sien**
feminine singular	**la mienne**	**la tienne**	**la sienne**
masculine plural	**les miens**	**les tiens**	**les siens**
feminine plural	**les miennes**	**les tiennes**	**les siennes**

and as follows when there is more than one possessor:

	ours	*yours* (**vous**)	*theirs*
masculine and feminine singular	**le/la nôtre**	**le/la vôtre**	**le/la leur**
masculine and feminine plural	**les nôtres**	**les vôtres**	**les leurs**

Possessive pronouns are used to avoid repeating a noun:

> Ma mère m'a prêté sa voiture parce que **la mienne** est chez le garagiste.   *My mother has lent me her car because mine is being repaired.*

- **Le, la**, and **les** combine with **de** and **à** in the usual way:

> J'ai besoin **du** tien.   *I need yours.*

17.4 À moi

Another common way of expressing possession is using a form of **être** + **à** + the appropriate emphatic pronoun (**moi, toi**, etc. See 28.2.5).

> Ce livre **est à moi**.   *This book is mine.*

Beware that **c'est à moi** can mean *it's mine* or *it's my turn* (see 28.2.5).

18 Demonstratives

Demonstratives are words like **ce** (*this*) or **celui-ci** (*this one*). They are used when pointing out something or someone.

18.1 Demonstrative Adjectives

Like all adjectives, a demonstrative adjective agrees in gender and number with the following noun. Its forms are:

Before a . . .			
masculine singular noun	ce	ce livre	*this/that book*
masculine singular noun starting with a vowel or silent **h**	cet	cet hôtel	*this/that hotel*
feminine singular noun	cette	cette maison	*this/that house*
masculine or feminine plural noun	ces	ces livres	*these/those books*

French rarely expresses any difference between *this* and *that*. However, when there is a need to make the difference, **-ci** is added after the noun to express that something is nearer (*this, these*), and **-là** to express that something is further away (*that, those*):

Ces pommes-**ci** sont douces, *These apples are sweet, those*
ces pommes-**là** sont acides. *apples are sour.*
J'étais absent ce jour-**là**. *I was not here on that day.*

18.2 Demonstrative Pronouns

■ 18.2.1 *Celui*

The pronoun **celui** means *the one*. Its different forms are:

	Singular	Plural
Masculine	**celui**	**ceux**
Feminine	**celle**	**celles**

Celui, celle, etc. are used:

- with a preposition (**à, de, devant, dans,** etc.) + noun:

  Vous voulez **celles** à   *Do you want the ones at*
  15 francs le kilo?   *15 francs a kilo?*
  Je préfère ta voiture à **celle** *I prefer your car to my*
  de mon père.   *father's.*

- with a relative pronoun:

  Celui qui me plaît le plus,   *The one I like most is*
  c'est Tom Cruise.   *Tom Cruise.*

- with **-ci** and **-là** to mean *this one, that one, these ones,* or *those ones*:

Masculine	Feminine	
celui-ci	**celle-ci**	*this one*
celui-là	**celle-là**	*that one*
ceux-ci	**celles-ci**	*these ones*
ceux-là	**celles-là**	*those ones*

Quelle couleur préférez-vous? *Which color do you prefer?*
Celle-ci ou **celle-là**?   *This one or that one?*

■ 18.2.2 *Ce*

Ce is the neutral form of **celui**. It is mainly used before a relative pronoun (**ce qui, ce que,** etc.; see 27.3) and in the expression **c'est** (*it is*) which is used:

- to define or identify things and people:
  C'est un ordinateur.   *It's a computer.*
  C'est ma sœur.   *She is my sister.*

- to express a judgment or a comment:
  Ce n'est pas grave.   *It's not serious. It doesn't matter.*

In this construction, when **être** is followed by a plural noun or pronoun, it is usually in the plural:

Ce sont des choses qui   *These things happen.*
arrivent.

■ 18.2.3 *Ceci, cela, ça*

Ceci (*this*) is not used very often in French, but **cela** and its contraction **ça**—used in informal spoken French—are very frequently used to mean both *this* and *that*.

Cela ne m'intéresse pas   *That/It doesn't interest me at all!*
du tout!

English speakers often find it difficult to decide whether to use **cela/ça** or **il/elle** for *it*. While **il/elle** refer back to the noun itself, **cela/ça** are used in a more general sense. For example, if you have just shown your friend around your new house you might say:

Elle te plaît?   *Do you like it?*

Or less specifically:

Ça te plaît?   *Do you like it?*

Indefinites are words like **chaque** (*each*), **autre** (*other*), and **certain** (*certain*). Most can be used either as an adjective:

Je l'ai vue l'**autre** jour.   *I saw her the other day.*

or as a pronoun:

Les **autres** viendront plus tard.   *The others will arrive later.*

19.1 Forms

A number of indefinite adjectives and pronouns have the same form:

autre(s)	*other, another one, other ones*
aucun(s), aucune(s)	*no, none*
certain(s), certaine(s)	*certain, some*
même(s)	*same*
nul(s), nulle(s)	*no, not any, no one*
plusieurs	*several*
tel(s), telle(s)	*such*
tout/tous, toute(s)	*all, everything*

A few indefinites have slightly different forms as adjectives and pronouns:

Adjectives		Pronouns	
chaque	*each*	**chacun(e)**	*each one*
quelque(s)	*some*	**quelqu'un**	*someone*
		quelques-un(e)s	*a few*

19.2 Use

■ 19.2.1 Agreement

Indefinite adjectives agree with the noun they describe and they normally come before the noun (**chaque** is an exception and doesn't agree):

Je n'ai **aucune** crainte.	*I have no fear.*
Elle est restée **quelques** jours.	*She stayed for a few days.*

Indefinite pronouns, except **quelqu'un**, agree with the noun they replace or represent:

Quelques-unes de ces pommes sont pourries.	*Some of these apples are rotten.*

■ 19.2.2 *Tout*

• Used as an adjective, **tout** is followed by the definite article (**le, la, les**) and means *all*, *every,* or *whole*:

tous les jours	*every day*	**toute la** journée	*all day*
toutes les fois	*every time*	**tout le** gâteau	*the whole cake*

Tous les/toutes les can also be used with a number to mean *both*, *the three of them*, etc.:

Ils sont venus **tous les** deux.	*They both came.*

• Used as a pronoun (i.e., not with a noun), **tout** means *everything*:

Je prends **tout**.	*I take everything.*

Tous and **toutes** mean *all*:

Ils viennent **tous**.	*They are all coming.*

■ 19.2.3 **Même** has various meanings:

J'irai le **même** jour.	*I'll go on the **same** day.*
J'irai le jour **même**.	*I'll go on that **very** day.*
J'irai **même** ce jour-là.	*I'll **even** go on that day.*
J'irai moi-**même**.	*I'll go my**self**.*

■ 19.2.4 **Tel** is usually preceded by an article:

Il fait une **telle** chaleur!	*It is so hot!* (literally, *such a heat*)

■ 19.2.5 **Quelque** is mostly used without an article:

Je ne les ai pas vus depuis **quelques** semaines.	*I haven't seen them for some weeks.*

Note that **quelque** is also used as an adverb with numbers—in which case it doesn't take an **-s**:

Quelque 2000 manifestants se sont rassemblés place Gambetta.	*About 2000 demonstrators gathered on Gambetta Square.*

■ **19.2.6 Autre** is normally used with an article:

Pas celui-ci, **l'autre.**	*Not this one, the other one.*
Je n'aime pas ce livre, j'en veux **un autre.**	*I don't like this book, I want another one.*

■ **19.2.7** When **aucun(e), un(e) autre, d'autres, certain(e)s, plusieurs,** and **quelques-un(e)s** are used as direct object pronouns, **en** must be used before the verb:

J'**en** ai acheté **quelques-uns.**	*I bought a few.*
Je n'**en** ai vu **aucun.**	*I haven't seen any.*

■ **19.2.8** When **personne, quelqu'un, quelque chose, rien,** and **plusieurs,** are followed by an adjective, **bien** or **mal, de** comes before the adjective, **bien** or **mal:**

C'est quelqu'un **de** bien.	*(S)he is very good.*
Vous avez mangé quelque chose **de** bon?	*Did you eat anything good?*
Rien **de** nouveau?	*Nothing new?*

20 Questions and Exclamations

20.1 Asking a Direct Question

In French there are three ways of asking the same question without a question word. For example, to ask someone *Do you have children?* you could:

- use the normal word order for a statement and raise your voice at the end:
  Vous avez des enfants?

- add **est-ce que** before the statement:
  Est-ce que vous avez des enfants?

- invert the verb and the subject pronoun:
  Avez-vous des enfants?

When using a question word, you also have these three options—though in the first option, the question word tends to come last. For example, for *Where do you work?* you can say:

- Vous travaillez **où**?

- **Où** est-ce que vous travaillez?

- **Où** travaillez-vous?

The first two word orders are used extensively in spoken French. The third one, normally called inversion, is still common with short verbs and pronouns, but on the whole tends to be used less and less and can sound quite formal. Note that when inverting, a -t- is added between the verb and the pronoun if the verb ends in a vowel and the pronoun starts with one:

  A-t-il des enfants?   *Does he have children?*

In spoken French the subject is often repeated by using both a noun and a pronoun, which may or may not be inverted:

  Vos enfants, ils sont toujours à l'école?   *Are your children*
  Vos enfants, sont-**ils** toujours à l'école?   *still at school?*

20.2 Asking *Who? What? Which?* etc.

■ **20.2.1** **Qui** is the question word for *who/whom* and **que** is the question word for *what*. They are used:

- on their own:
  Qui a appelé?   *Who called?*
  Que faites-vous?   *What are you doing?*

- or, if **qui/que** is the subject, combined with **est-ce qui**:
  Qui est-ce qui manque?   *Who is missing?*
  Qu'est-ce qui se passe?   *What is happening?*

- or, if **qui/que** is the object, with **est-ce que**:
  Qui est-ce que vous avez   *Whom did you meet?*
  rencontré?
  Qu'est-ce que vous désirez?   ***What*** *do you want?*

See 20.2.4 for when to use **quoi** instead of **que**.

■ **20.2.2** **Quel** is the question word for *which* or *what* when followed by a noun. It agrees with the noun it refers to.

	Masculine	Feminine
Singular	quel	quelle
Plural	quels	quelles

    Quel jour venez-vous?   *Which day will you be coming?*
    Quelle est votre adresse?   *What is your address?*

■ **20.2.3** **Lequel** is the question word for *which one*. It agrees with the noun it refers to.

	Masculine	Feminine
Singular	lequel	laquelle
Plural	lesquels	lesquelles

Regarde ces chaussures.	*Look at these shoes.*
Lesquelles préfères-tu?	*Which ones do you prefer?*

The forms **lequel, lesquels,** and **lesquelles** combine with **à** and **de** (see 27.1):

Auquel pensez-vous?	*Which one are you thinking of?*

■ 20.2.4 *What with? Who with?* etc.

Qui combines with a preposition to mean *with whom?, for whom?*, etc. **Quoi** is used instead of **que** with a preposition to mean *with what?, of what?*, etc. The preposition comes first:

Avec quoi l'as-tu fait?	*What did you do it with?*
Pour qui est-ce que vous travaillez?	*Whom do you work for?*

■ 20.2.5 Other uses of *Quoi?* and *Comment?*

Note that **Comment?** is often used on its own to ask someone to repeat something.

Quoi? is used in very informal French:

- like **Comment?** to express that you haven't heard very well or clearly

- and in the expression **C'est quoi?** which is an informal equivalent to **Qu'est-ce que c'est?** (*What is it?*):
  C'est quoi, la tarte Tatin?   *What is a tarte Tatin?*

20.3 Indirect Questions

An indirect question comes after a verb like **demander** (*to ask*), **dire** (*to tell*), **savoir** (*to know*), or **se demander** (*to wonder*). It does not have a question mark at the end:

Je ne sais pas **ce qui se passe.**	*I don't know what is going on.*
Je me demande **s'ils vont venir.**	*I wonder whether they will come.*

An inversion can occur in an indirect question. It happens when the subject is a noun and when the verb would otherwise be the last word of the sentence. Compare:

Je ne sais pas **à quelle heure part le train.**	*I don't know at what time the train is leaving.*
Je ne sais pas **à quelle heure il part.**	*I don't know at what time it leaves.*

20.4 Exclamations

Exclamations are a way to express a reaction to something: surprise, admiration, disgust, etc. For exclamations, you may use:

Que

Qu'il fait chaud!	*It's so hot!*

Comme (not used as often as **que**)

Comme c'est beau!	*It's so beautiful!/How beautiful it is!*

Quel(s), quelle(s) + noun

Quel temps!	*What weather!*

21 Negatives

The most common pattern for negations in French is
ne/n' + verb + **pas**, **rien**, **plus**, etc.:

| Je **n'irai pas** demain. | *I will not/I won't be going tomorrow.* |
| Je **ne comprends rien**. | *I don't understand anything.* |

See 8.1, 10.1 for the use of **de** after a negative.

21.1 The Main Negatives

The most common negatives are:

ne... pas	*not*
ne... rien	*nothing/not anything*
ne... plus	*no more/not any more/* *no longer/not any longer*
ne... jamais	*never*
ne... personne	*no one/nobody/not anyone*
ne... aucun(e)	*no/not any/none*
ne... guère	*hardly*
ne... ni... ni	*neither . . . nor*
ne... nulle part	*nowhere*
ne... que	*only*

| Il **ne fait plus** de piano. | *He no longer plays the piano.* |
| Il **n'y a personne** dans la bibliothèque. | *There is no one in the library.* |

Some of the above negatives can be combined. For example:

Il **n'y a plus rien**.	*There is nothing left.*
Il **n'aime pas** ça, et moi **non plus**.	*He doesn't like it, and neither do I.*
Il **n'y avait pas que** lui.	*He was not the only one.*

21.2 Position of Negatives

■ **21.2.1** Ne always comes before the verb and object pronouns, while **pas**, **plus**, **rien**, etc. come after the verb:

| Je **ne** le lui demanderai **pas**. | *I won't ask him/her.* |

Note that **que** (*only*) and **ni** (*neither*) come just before the word they refer to and therefore not always just after the verb:

Il **ne** fait du piano **que** deux fois par semaine.	*He only plays the piano twice a week.*
Je **ne** veux boire **ni** du vin **ni** de la bière.	*I don't want to drink wine or beer.*

■ **21.2.2** In compound tenses **pas, plus, rien, jamais,** and **guère** come just after the **avoir/être** form:

Elle n'**a rien** remarqué.	*She didn't notice anything.*
Je ne l'**ai jamais** vu.	*I have never seen it.*

But **aucun(e), personne,** and **que** come after the participle:

Nous n'avons **vu personne.**	*We haven't seen anyone.*
Je n'ai **fait que** la vaisselle.	*I have only done the washing up.*

With **ne... ni... ni**, each **ni** comes just before the word or phrase it refers to:

Il n'a **ni** bu **ni** mangé.	*He has neither drunk nor eaten.*
Je n'ai parlé **ni** à la directrice **ni** à son assistant.	*I didn't talk to the manager nor to her assistant.*

■ **21.2.3** When a negation refers to an infinitive, both parts come together before the infinitive:

Il espère **ne pas avoir** de retard.	*He hopes not to be late.*

This construction occurs with **ne... pas, ne... plus, ne... rien, ne... jamais,** and **ne... guère**. The other negatives enclose the infinitive:

J'ai décidé de **ne recevoir personne**.	*I have decided not to receive anyone.*

■ **21.2.4 Negatives at the Beginning of a Sentence**
Some negatives can be placed before the verb. In this case, the second part of the negative (**personne**, **rien**, **aucun**, etc.) comes first, followed by **ne** and the verb:

Personne n'a téléphoné?	*Has no one phoned?*
Jamais je n'achèterais une si grosse voiture!	*I would never buy such a big car!*

21.3 Leaving Out *ne*

Note that **ne** is never used when there is no verb:

Pas moi!	*Not me!*
Moi non plus!	*Neither do I!*

It is also often left out in informal spoken French:

Tu vas pas au bureau?	*Aren't you going to the office?*

21.4 Leaving Out *pas*

Pas is usually left out after **cesser** (*to stop*), and sometimes after **pouvoir** (*to be able*), **savoir** (*to know*), and **oser** (*to dare*):

Il n'a cessé de pleuvoir.	*It didn't stop raining.*
Je n'ai pu le convaincre.	*I was not able to convince him.*
Il ne sait que faire.	*He doesn't know what to do.*
Ils n'osent le lui dire.	*They don't dare tell him.*

Pas is also sometimes left out in a **si** clause that expresses a condition:

Si je ne me trompe, c'est au dernier étage.	*If I am not mistaken, it's on the top floor.*

21.5 Other Uses of *ne*

In careful speech, **ne** is used in a few cases for stylistic reasons without having a negative meaning:

- in comparisons, after **plus... que, moins... que**:

  C'est plus grave qu'ils **ne** pensent.   *It is more serious than they think.*

- after a few conjunctions taking the subjunctive (see 49.2), **avant que** (*before*), **à moins que** (*unless*), **de crainte que** (*for fear that*), and **de peur que** (*for fear that*):

  Je vais faire quelques courses **avant que** les magasins **ne** ferment.   *I'll go and do some shopping before the stores close.*

- after verbs expressing fear, such as **avoir peur que** and **craindre que**:

  Je **crains qu'il ne** soit trop tard!   *I fear it might be too late!*

Leaving out **ne** in the above cases does not affect the meaning of the sentence. It just makes it sound less formal.

22 Subject Pronouns

The subject pronouns are:

Singular		Plural	
je/j'	I	nous	we
tu	you	vous	you
il	he/it	ils	they
elle	she/it	elles	they
on	one/we/they		

22.1 Je

Je changes to **j'** before a vowel or a silent **h**:

    J'habite à Chicago.   *I live in Chicago.*

22.2 Tu and Vous

Tu and **vous** both mean *you*:

- **Tu** is used when talking to one person who is a relative, a friend, or a young person.

- **Vous** is used to talk to one person more formally, or to more than one person.

    Pierre et Catherine, **vous**   *Pierre and Catherine,*
    voulez un café?   *would you like coffee?*

22.3 Il/Elle, Ils/Elles

These pronouns refer to people, animals, and things. They agree in gender and number with the noun they replace.

    La nouvelle **voiture**, **elle** te plaît? *Do you like the new car?*

Ils is used when referring to several nouns of different genders:

    Je prends ce lit et cette   *I'll take this bed and this*
    armoire; **ils** me plaisent.   *chest of drawers; I like them.*

Il is also used as a neutral pronoun in certain phrases and with some verbs—a few of which, like **pleuvoir** (*to rain*) and **falloir** (*to have to*), can only be used in the **il** form (see Impersonal Verbs, 46):

Il y a des gens qui sont contre.	*There are people who are against it.*
Il vaut mieux partir tôt.	*It is better to leave early.*

22.4 *On*

On is used:

- as *people* or *you* are sometimes used in English:

En France, **on** roule à droite.	*In France, you drive on the right.*

- for *someone* when the identity of the subject is not relevant; in English, a passive form is often used:

On m'a dit qu'il fallait réserver.	*I was told to reserve in advance.*

- instead of **nous**—this is very common in spoken French. The verb is in the singular:

On va au cinéma ce soir?	*Shall we go to the movies tonight?*

In compound tenses, the past participle may be singular or plural:

On est **arrivé(s/es)** très tard.	*We arrived very late.*

After conjunctions like **si** (*if*), **lorsque** (*when*), **qui** (*who*), **quoi** (*what*), **et** (*and*), **ou** (*or*), **où** (*where*), **que** (*that, which*), etc. **l'** is sometimes placed before **on**. It bears no meaning and is there only to make pronunciation easier:

Je ne savais pas que **l'on** pouvait réserver par Minitel.	*I didn't know one could make reservations through Minitel.*

23 Object Pronouns

Object pronouns are either the direct or the indirect object of the verb:

Je **le** vois demain. *I am seeing **him** tomorrow. (Direct)*

Je **lui** parlerai. *I'll talk **to him/her**. (Indirect)*

23.1 Forms

Some direct and indirect object pronouns have the same form:

me, m'	(*me/to me*)	**nous**	(*us/to us*)
te, t'	(*you/to you*)	**vous**	(*you/to you*)

In the third person the indirect pronouns have a different form from the direct pronouns:

Direct object pronouns		Indirect object pronouns	
le, l'	(*him/it*)	**lui**	(*to him/to her/to it*)
la, l'	(*her/it*)	**leur**	(*to them*)
les	(*them*)		

Me, te, le, and **la** change to **m', t',** and **l'** before a vowel or a silent **h**:

Je **l'ai**. *I have it.*

Moi and **toi** are used instead of **me** and **te** when they come after the verb and they are not followed by **en**. This happens in the positive imperative (see 41.2):

Envoyez-le-**moi**! *Send it to me!*

Envoyez-**m'en** trois! *Send me three.*

But:

Ne **me** l'envoyez pas! *Don't send it to me!*

23.2 Direct or Indirect Pronoun?

A direct object pronoun replaces a direct object. It answers the question **qui est-ce que...?** (*whom . . . ?*) or **qu'est-ce que...?** (*what . . . ?*).

Je lis **ce livre**.	*I am reading **this book**.*
Je **le** lis.	*I am reading **it**.*
J'ai vu **mon frère**.	*I have seen **my brother**.*
Je **l'**ai vu.	*I have seen **him**.*

An indirect object pronoun usually refers to a person. It answers the question **à qui?** (*to whom?*):

J'ai donné le ticket **à mon frère**.	*I gave the ticket **to my brother**.*
Je **lui** ai donné le ticket.	*I gave **him** the ticket.*

■ **23.2.1** Note that some verbs take a direct object in French while their English equivalents take an indirect object, for example **attendre** (*to wait for*), **demander** (*to ask for*), etc. (see 47.1):

Je **l'**attendrai.	*I will wait for him.*
Je **l'**ai cherché partout.	*I have looked for it everywhere.*

■ **23.2.2** A few verbs take an indirect object where the English takes a direct object (see 47.2.2 for list):

Je **lui** ai demandé de m'aider.	*I asked him/her to help me.*
Je **leur** ai téléphoné hier.	*I phoned them yesterday.*

23.3 Word Order of Object Pronouns

Object pronouns come just before the verb and in compound tenses, just before the auxiliary:

Vous ne **le** voyez plus?	*Don't you see him any more?*
Je **lui** ai parlé.	*I have talked to him/her.*

When there are two verbs, the pronoun comes just before the verb it refers to:

Je vais **le** faire.　　　*I am going to do it.*

A direct and an indirect object pronoun can be used together in front of the verb in the following two combinations:

1	2
me	le
te	la
nous	les
vous	

or

1	2
le	lui
la	leur
les	nous
	vous

Il **me le** donne.　　　*He gives it to me.*
Il **le lui** a vendu.　　*He has sold it to him.*

But in affirmative commands, the direct object comes before the indirect and is linked to the verb by a hyphen:

Donne-**le-leur**!　　*Give it to them!*

En and **y** are also object pronouns (see 24 and 25). The following table summarizes the order in which object pronouns appear before a verb:

	1	2	3	4	5	
subject (ne)	me te nous vous	le la les	lui leur	y	en	verb (**pas, plus,** etc.)

Nous **lui en** avons parlé.　*We have talked to him about it.*
Je **l'y** ai envoyé.　　　　　*I have sent him there.*

24 *En*

The pronoun **en** is used in a variety of constructions and with several meanings.

24.1 Uses of *en*

■ **24.1.1** The pronoun **en** replaces a noun introduced by **de, du, de la,** or **des.** If translated at all, it can mean *some* or *any*:

J'ai fait du café. Vous **en** voulez?	*I have made some coffee. Would you like some?*
Je n'**en** prends pas, merci.	*I won't have any, thank you.*

■ **24.1.2** **En** is often used with expressions of quantity. It avoids repetition of the thing you are talking about. It is rarely translated in English:

Il y a **assez de** tomates?	*Are there enough tomatoes?*
Oui, il y **en a une livre**.	*Yes, there is a pound (of them).*

En is also used with numbers and with some indefinite pronouns :

Combien **en** voulez-vous?	*How many (of them) do you*
J'**en** veux **deux**.	*want? I want two.*
Il y **en** avait **quelques-uns**.	*There were a few (of them).*

■ **24.1.3** **En** can also stand for the name of a place introduced by **de** (meaning *from*); it then has the meaning of *from there*:

Tu es allé à la poste?	*Have you been to the post office?*
Oui, j'**en** viens.	*I have just come from there.*

■ **24.1.4** With verbs or verbal phrases that are followed by **de** (**avoir besoin de**, *to need*; etc. see 47.3), **en** stands for the noun or phrase introduced by **de**:

Tu peux prendre la voiture.	*You can take the car. I don't*
Je n'**en** ai pas besoin.	*need it.*

Instead of:

Je n'ai pas besoin **de la voiture**. *I don't need **the car**.*

En cannot be used to refer to a person:

| Je ne veux pas qu'il vienne: | *I don't want him to come:* |
| je n'ai pas besoin de lui. | *I don't need him.* |

■ **24.1.5 En** is used with adjectives that are followed by **de** (see 13.1). Most of these adjectives express either an emotion (**content de**, *pleased*; **ravi de**, *delighted with*), an ability (**capable de**, *capable of*), or a certitude (**certain de**, *certain of*; **sûr de**, *sure of*):

| Nous **en** sommes ravis. | *We are delighted about it.* |
| J'**en** suis sûr. | *I am sure of it.* |

Here too it is preferable not to use **en** when referring to a person:

Je suis fier d'elle. *I am proud of her.*

■ **24.1.6 En** is also used in some colloquial expressions. Some of the most common are noted below:

s'**en** aller	*to go away*
s'**en** faire	*to worry*
en vouloir à	*to be cross with*
en avoir assez	*to have had enough*
en avoir marre	*to be fed up*
Je **m'en vais**.	*I am going.*
Allez-vous **en**!	*Go away!*
Ne vous **en faites** pas!	*Don't worry!*

24.2 Position of *en*

Like the other object pronouns, **en** comes before the verb, except when used in a positive command:

N'**en** prends pas! *Don't take any!*

but:

   Prends-**en** deux!   *Have two!*

When used with other object pronouns, **en** comes last,
whether before or after the verb (see 23.3):

   Il n'**y en** a pas assez.   *There isn't enough.*
   Ne **m'en** donnez pas!   *Don't give me any!*
   Donnez-**m'en** une livre.   *Give me a pound (of it).*

25.1 Uses of y

■ **25.1.1** Y is used to mean *there*. It avoids repetition of a noun introduced by **à**, **sur**, **dans**, **chez**, or another preposition of location:

Tu vas au bureau? Oui, j'**y** vais dans cinq minutes.	*Are you going to the office? Yes, I am going (there) in five minutes.*
Vous allez chez le médecin? Oui, j'**y** vais demain.	*Are you going to the doctor's? Yes, I am going tomorrow.*

Y is often used with **aller** even when no particular place is mentioned:

Allons-**y**!	*Let's go!*
On **y** va?	*Shall we go?*

Note the following expressions:

Ça **y** est!	*That's it!*
Nous **y** voilà!/On **y** est!	*Here we are!*

■ **25.1.2** Y is also used to avoid repeating a noun or phrase introduced by **à**. For example after **arriver à** (*to manage to*), **s'attendre à** (*to expect to*), and **penser à** (*to think about*):

Je n'**y** arrive pas.	*I can't manage to do it.*
Je m'**y** attendais.	*I was expecting it to happen.*
Tu **y** as pensé?	*Did you think about that?*

Like **en**, y cannot be used to refer to a person:

J'ai beaucoup pensé à elle.	*I thought a lot about her.*

25.2 Position of y

Like **en**, **y** is placed before the verb, except in positive commands. It comes after other object pronouns but comes before **en** (see 23.3):

Il **y en** a un peu.	*There is a little bit (of it).*

26 Reflexive and Emphatic Pronouns

26.1 Reflexive Pronouns

Reflexive pronouns are used in reflexive verbs (see 45) and, also, in the plural, with the meaning of *each other*:

| Nous nous sommes levés de bonne heure. | *We got up early.* |
| Ils se téléphonent tous les jours. | *They phone each other every day.* |

These are the forms:

Singular	Plural
me *myself*	**nous** *ourselves/each other*
te *yourself*	**vous** *yourselves/each other*
se *himself/herself/itself*	**se** *themselves/each other*

26.2 Emphatic Pronouns

Emphatic pronouns, also called disjunctive pronouns, are used particularly for emphasis or after a preposition.

| Moi, je n'aime pas ça! | *I don't like that!* |
| Je peux venir avec toi? | *Can I come with you?* |

These are the forms:

Singular	Plural
moi *I/me*	**nous** *we/us*
toi *you*	**vous** *you*
lui *he/him*	**eux** *they/them* (masculine)
elle *she/her*	**elles** *they/them* (feminine)
soi *oneself*	

■ 26.2.1 Use

Emphatic pronouns are used:

- for emphasis. They are used to stress a pronoun, in which case the emphatic pronoun comes first:

Lui, il est homme au foyer et **elle,** elle est PDG.	He is a house husband and she is a managing director.

  or a noun, in which case the emphatic pronoun comes after the noun:

J'ai un mauvais rhume, mais les enfants, **eux,** sont en pleine forme.	I have a bad cold, but the children are fine.

- on their own. Emphatic pronouns are often used in answers where no verb is needed:

Qui veut y aller? Pas **moi!**	Who wants to go there? Not me!

- after **c'est, ce sont:**

Qui est là? C'est **moi!**	Who's there? It's I!
Ce sont **eux?**	Is it they?

- after a preposition:

J'étais assise devant **lui.**	I was sitting in front of him.
C'est à **elle!**	It's her turn./It's hers.

Emphatic pronouns are used with verbal phrases followed by **de** or **à** to refer to persons, while **en** and **y** are used to refer to things or ideas (see 24.1.4/5 and 25.1.2):

J'ai besoin **de vous.**	I need you.
J'**en** ai besoin.	I need it.
Je pense **à lui.**	I am thinking of him.
J'**y** pense.	I am thinking about it.

- with **-même(s)** (*-self, -selves*), **aussi** (*too*), and **seul** (*alone*):

Ils l'ont fait **eux-mêmes.**	They have done it by themselves/on their own.

Toi aussi, tu en veux?	*Would you like some too?*
Lui seul peut le faire.	*He alone can do it.*

- in a comparison:

Tu es plus malin que **moi**!	*You are more clever than I am!*

- before a relative pronoun:

C'est **toi** qui as appelé il y a dix minutes?	*Did you phone (Is it you who phoned) ten minutes ago?*

- with a noun:

Ma femme et **moi** aimerions vous inviter à dîner.	*My wife and I would like to invite you for dinner.*
Je les vois souvent, **lui** et ses enfants.	*I often see him and his children.*

26.3 Use of *Soi*

Soi (*oneself*) is used in general statements to refer to indefinite pronouns like **chacun** (*each one*), **tout le monde** (*everyone*), **personne** (*nobody*), etc.:

Chacun est rentré chez **soi**.	*Each went home.*
Cela va de **soi**.	*It goes without saying.*

27 Relative Pronouns

Relative pronouns are pronouns that link a noun or a pronoun with a clause, for example, **la voiture** *qui*... (*the car which/that* . . .), **l'homme** *qui*... (*the man who* . . .), **celle** *que*... (*the one which/that* . . .), **la maison devant** *laquelle* (*the house in front of which*), etc.

27.1 Forms

The relative pronouns are:

qui	*who/which/that*	**quoi**	*what*
que	*whom/which/that*	**dont**	*whose/of which*
ce qui	*what*	**où**	*where/when*
ce que	*what*		

and the various forms of **lequel**:

	Singular	Plural
Masculine	**lequel**	**lesquels**
Feminine	**laquelle**	**lesquelles**

Lequel, etc. combine with the prepositions **à** and **de**, except in the feminine singular:

à + lequel	**auquel**	**de + lequel**	**duquel**
à + lesquels	**auxquels**	**de + lesquels**	**desquels**
à + lesquelles	**auxquelles**	**de + lesquelles**	**desquelles**
but	**à laquelle**	but	**de laquelle**

27.2 *Qui* and *Que*

Qui (*who, which, that*) and **que** (*whom, which, that*) are used to link a noun or a pronoun with the next clause. They can refer to people *or* things. **Qui** is the subject of the following verb:

la personne **qui arrive**...	*the person who is coming . . .*
la voiture **qui arrive**...	*the car which is arriving . . .*
la personne **que tu vois**...	*the person whom you can see . . .*
la voiture **que tu vois**...	*the car that you can see . . .*

and **que/qui** is the object:

| C'est une zone **qui** est en pleine expansion. | *This is a zone which is in full expansion.* |
| Le conseil d'administration **que** M. Bolloré devait présider, a été remis. | *The board meeting that Mr. Bolloré was due to preside over, has been postponed.* |

Note that:

- the verb following **qui** agrees with the noun or pronoun which **qui** stands for:

  | C'est **moi qui fais** la vaisselle. | *I'll do (or I do) the cleanup.* |

- **que**, when it means *whom* or *that*, cannot be omitted as it can be in English:

  | La commande **qu'ils** ont passée hier, est très importante. | *The order they placed yesterday is considerable.* |

27.3 Ce qui, Ce que

Ce qui and **ce que** mean *what*. **Ce qui** is used when it is the subject and **ce que** when it is the object of the following verb:

ce qui = subject	ce que/qu' = object
Je ne sais pas **ce qui** est arrivé. *I don't know what has happened.*	Je ne sais pas **ce qu'il** a dit. *I don't know what he said.*

Ce **qui** and ce **que** are used in a general sense, when there is no specific item or person to refer to. Compare these two sentences:

Je ne comprends pas **le mot qu'**il a laissé.	*I don't understand the note that he left behind.*
Je ne comprends pas **ce qu'**il a écrit.	*I don't understand what he has written.*

Note also that ce **qui** and ce **que** are used after **tout** for *everything that*:

Je ne suis pas d'accord avec tout **ce qu'**il a dit.	*I don't agree with everything (that) he said.*

27.4 Preposition Followed by a Relative Pronoun

The relative pronoun after a preposition is either **qui** or **lequel** or **quoi**.

■ **27.4.1** When the relative pronoun refers to a person, **qui** is used in most cases:

J'ai trouvé un opticien chez **qui** je vais travailler en août.	*I have found an optician whom I am going to work for in August.*

It is however possible to use **lequel**:

Le patron pour **lequel** je travaille, est très sympathique.	*The boss I am working for is very friendly.*

After **entre** and **parmi** only **lequel** can be used:

Il avait 32 élèves, **parmi lesquels** certains étaient très doués.	*He had 32 students, some of whom were very gifted.*

■ **27.4.2** When the relative pronoun refers to a thing or an idea, **qui** cannot be used. In most cases **lequel** is used:

C'est **un argument auquel** nos clients sont de plus en plus sensibles.	*It is an argument that increasingly appeals to our clients (to which our clients are becoming more and more sensitive).*

When the relative pronoun does not refer to a specific noun, **quoi** is used after a preposition:

Je ne sais pas **avec quoi** elle l'a fait.	*I don't know what she did it with.*

27.5 *Dont*

Dont (*of which, of whom, whose*) is used instead of **de qui**. The word order is: **dont** + subject + verb + object, which is quite different from the English construction.

Voici Daniel **dont** tu as rencontré les beaux-parents la semaine dernière.	*This is Daniel, whose parents-in-law you met last week.*

It is used:

*   to mean *whose*:

Nous avons beaucoup d'élèves **dont** les parents sont au chômage.	*We have many pupils whose parents are unemployed.*

*   to mean *of which*:

On a commencé à construire le pont **dont** il a fait les plans.	*They have started to build the bridge which he made the plans of.*

*   with verbs and adjectives which take **de** (see 13.1 and 47.3):

Voilà les amis **dont** je vous ai parlé.	*Here are my friends I talked to you about.*

Le projet **dont** nous nous sommes occupés, a eu beaucoup de succès.	*The project we dealt with has been very successful.*
C'est la seule chose **dont** je suis sûr.	*It's the only thing I am sure of.*

When **dont** does not refer to a specific noun, it is preceded by **ce** or **tout ce**:

Nous nous ferons un plaisir de vous procurer **tout ce** dont vous aurez besoin.	*It will be a pleasure to provide you with everything you might need.*

27.6 *Où*

Où is used:

- to mean *where*:

Le restaurant **où** nous allons déjeuner, est très sympathique.	*The restaurant where we will be having lunch is very nice.*

- to mean *in/to/on/at which*:

La maison **où** ils habitent, est à vendre.	*The house in which they live is for sale.*

- to mean *when*, after a noun referring to time:

Il pleuvait **le jour où** nous sommes arrivés.	*It was raining on the day we arrived.*
Il a enlevé sa main juste **au moment où** la porte se refermait.	*He took his hand away just as the door closed.*

28 Prepositions

Prepositions are words like **sous** (*under*) or **dans** (*in*). In this section, we will concentrate on the most important ones.

28.1 Using the Right Preposition

■ 28.1.1 With Geographical Names

- With the name of a town **à** is always used, regardless of whether you mean *to* or *in*:

Je suis **à** Paris.	*I am in Paris.*
Je vais **à** Paris.	*I go to Paris.*

- With the name of a country, continent, or region, its gender determines whether you use **en**, **au**, or **aux**— they all mean *to* or *in* depending on the context:

- Use **en** when the name of the country, continent, département, or region is feminine (i.e., if its name ends in -e):

J'habite **en France**.	*I live in France.*
Ils vont **en Australie**.	*They're going to Australia.*
La maison est **en Dordogne**.	*The house is in the Dordogne.*

  and when the name starts with a vowel: **en Israël, en Iran**.

- Use **au** with masculine names of countries (i.e., names not ending in -e): **au Canada, au Japon, au Kenya, au Pérou**, and when the name of a town starts with **Le: au Havre**.

- Use **aux** when the name is in the plural: **aux États-Unis** (*in the United States*), **aux Pays-Bas** (*in the Netherlands*).

- Use **dans** with names of mountain ranges: **dans les Alpes** (*in the Alpes*), and with départements whose name comes from a river that is masculine: **dans le Tarn** (*in Tarn*).

■ 28.1.2 With Means of Transport

En can be used with most means of transport:

en voiture	*by car*
en bus	*by bus*
en car	*by coach*
en vélo	*by bike*
en bicyclette	*by bicycle*
en avion	*by plane*
en train	*by train*

But say:

à pied	*on foot*

■ 28.1.3 With Months, Seasons, and Years

en janvier	*in January*
en été	*in summer*
en automne	*in autumn*
en hiver	*in winter*
en 1998	*in 1998*

but:

au printemps	*in spring*

■ 28.1.4 *À*, **en**, **vers**, etc. are used in expressions of time.

Compare these sentences:

Venez **à** 4 heures.	*Come at four o'clock.*
Venez **vers** 4 heures.	*Come at about four o'clock.*
Il vient **à** Noël.	*He is coming at Christmas.*
À demain!	*See you tomorrow!*
À lundi!	*See you on Monday!*

but:

Il vient lundi.	*He is coming on Monday.*
Il vient **le** 5 mai.	*He is coming on May 5th.*
Elle travaille **de** 8 heures **à** midi.	*She works from 8 o'clock till noon.*

Elle est à Paris **du** 1er **au** 3 mars.	*She'll be in Paris from March 1st to the 3rd.*
Elle restera **jusqu'à** vingt heures.	*She'll stay until 8 p.m.*
Elle restera **jusqu'au** 30 du mois.	*She'll stay until the 30th of the month.*

Je les vois deux fois **par** semaine. *I see them twice a week.*

Je l'ai fait **en** une heure.	*I did it in an hour.*
Téléphonez-moi **dans** une heure.	*Phone me in an hour's time.*

28.2 À

À has a wide range of uses. Note that it combines with the articles **le** and **les** as follows:

à + le = au   **à + les = aux**

■ **28.2.1** À can be used before the name of a place to describe a movement to that place (*to*):

Je vais **à la** maison.	*I am going home.*
Elle va **au** bureau.	*She is going to the office.*

or the position the location of a place (*at* or *in*):

Je suis **à la** maison.	*I am at home.*
Elle est **au** bureau.	*She is at the office.*

Also note the use of **à**:

• with names of towns:

Je vais **à** Montréal.	*I am going to Montreal.*

• to express distances:

C'est **à** 2 km.	*It is 2 km (about 1¼ miles) away.*

• to express density or speed:

1000 habitants **au** km².	*1000 inhabitants per km²*
	(247 acres).
Je fais du 90 km **à** l'heure.	*I am driving at 90 km (about*
	56 miles) per hour.

• and in many expressions such as:

à gauche	*on/to the left*
à droite	*on/to the right*

Note that **à** is often translated by *on*:

au premier étage	*on the first floor*
C'est **à** la page 5.	*It's on page 5.*
Qu'est-ce qu'il y a **au** menu?	*What is on the menu?*
C'est **à** l'ordre du jour.	*It's on the agenda.*
Qui est **à** l'appareil?	*Who is on the phone/*
	speaking?
Qu'est-ce qu'il y a **à** la	*What is on television/the*
télévision/radio?	*radio?*

■ **28.2.2 À Before the Indirect Object**
Some verbs can have an indirect object (see 47.2) that is
introduced by **à**:

J'en ai parlé **à** mes parents.	*I have talked to my parents*
	about it.

■ **28.2.3 À** may be used to add a qualifying or descriptive
element. It is used to:

• specify the nature or the type of an object:

un verre **à** vin	*a wine glass*

• add a description:

la fille **aux** cheveux longs	*the girl with the long hair*
des chaussures **à** hauts talons	*high-heeled shoes*

• specify a dish:

une tarte **aux** pommes	*an apple pie*
une escalope **à** la crème	*a veal cutlet with cream*

- specify a price:

Je voudrais celle **à** $10.   *I'd like the one at $10.*

■ **28.2.4 À** may be used to express manner:

On se chauffe **au** gaz.   *We have gas heating.*

C'est fait **à** la main.   *It's handmade.*

■ **28.2.5** In the phrase c'est à moi, c'est à lui, etc., à:

- either expresses possession:

C'est à toi? Non, **c'est à**   *Is it yours? No, it's my*
mon frère.   *brother's.*

- or expresses whose turn it is:

C'est à moi de faire la vaisselle.   *It's my turn to wash up.*

- or states whose responsibility something is:

C'est à tes parents de le   *It's your parents who should*
lui dire.   *tell him.*

■ **28.2.6 À After Certain Verbs and Adjectives**

The preposition **à** can follow certain verbs (see 47.2) and adjectives (see 13.2):

Je n'arrive pas **à** ouvrir cette   *I can't open this bottle.*
bouteille.

C'est difficile **à** traduire   *It is difficult to translate into*
en français.   *French.*

28.3 *En*

En is never followed by an article: **en ville** (*in town*).

■ **28.3.1 En** can mean *to, at,* or *in*:

- in a few expressions like **en ville** (*in/to town*), **en mer**
(*at sea*), **en montagne** (*in/to the mountains*)

- with names of countries that are feminine, i.e., which end in **-e** (**en Suisse**, *in Switzerland*, see 28.1.1).

■ **28.3.2 En** is used to express what something is made of:
un sac **en** cuir   *a leather bag*

■ **28.3.3 En** is used for some descriptions and in various expressions:

Il était **en** shorts.	*He was wearing shorts.*
Elle était toute **en** noir.	*She was wearing black.*
Je suis **en** bonne santé.	*I am in good health.*
en vacances	*on vacation*
être **en** panne	*to have a breakdown (of a vehicle)*
être **en** retard	*to be late*
en français	*in French*

■ **28.3.4 En** can be followed by a present participle (see 40.1.2):
J'ai écouté les nouvelles tout **en repassant**.   *I listened to the news while doing the ironing.*

28.4 *De*

De combines with **le** and **les** as follows:
de + le = du   **de + les = des**

■ **28.4.1 De** can mean *from*:

Vous êtes **de** Marseille?	*Are you from Marseilles?*
Vous venez **d'**où?	*Where do you come from?*
Il était ici **de** 2 à 4 heures.	*He was here from 2 till 4.*

■ **28.4.2 De** means *of* when it links two nouns (see 17.1). The English construction is usually very different:
Où sont les clefs **de** la voiture?   *Where are the car keys?*

Tu as lu la lettre **de** Paul?	*Did you read Paul's letter?*
J'ai rangé les affaires **des** enfants.	*I have tidied up the children's things.*
C'est un trajet **de** deux heures.	*It is a two-hour journey.*

■ **28.4.3** De is used in expressions of quantity. Beware that **de**—and never **des**—is used:

Il y a beaucoup **de** touristes.	*There are lots of tourists.*

■ **28.4.4** Note that **de**—and not **que**—is used:

• with **plus/moins** and a number:

Elle gagne plus **de** 10 000 F par mois.	*She earns more than 10,000 francs a month.*

• with **plus/moins/autant/davantage** and a noun:

Il y a davantage **de** monde que l'année dernière.	*There are more people than last year.*

• after a superlative:

C'est le plus petit pays **d'**Europe.	*It is the smallest country in Europe.*

■ **28.4.5** When **être** is used for stating a price or a measurement, **de** follows it:

Le prix est **de** $195.	*The price is $195.*
La profondeur est **de** 2 m 50.	*The depth is 2 m 50 (about 8 feet).*

■ **28.4.6** De is used in many expressions that:

• describe how something is or was done:

Je l'ai fait **d'**un seul coup.	*I did it in one try.*
Il m'a parlé **de** façon agressive.	*He spoke to me aggressively.*

* explain the reason why:

  Il était rouge **de** honte.   *He was red with shame.*

  Ils tremblaient **de** peur.   *They were shivering with fear.*

■ **28.4.7** De is used to link **quelque chose, rien, quelqu'un,** and **personne** with an adjective or **bien/mal**:

Tu as vu quelque chose   *Did you see anything nice?*
de bien?

C'est quelqu'un **de** bien.   *It is somebody nice.*

■ **28.4.8** De is also used after certain verbs (see 47.3) and after some adjectives (see 13.1):

Il m'a demandé **de** l'aider.   *He has asked me to help him.*

Je suis ravie **de** vous voir.   *I am delighted to see you.*

Il est facile **de** se tromper.   *It is easy to make a mistake.*

28.5 *Depuis, Pendant,* and *Il y a*

Depuis and **pendant** both mean *for* or *since* according to the context, while **il y a** means *ago*.

■ **28.5.1** Depuis is used:

* when talking about something that started in the past and is still going on. The verb is in the present tense:

  J'habite ici **depuis** 3 ans.   *I have been living here for 3 years.*

  Elle est aux États-Unis   *She has been in the United*
  depuis le 3 mars.   *States since March 3rd.*

* to express how long since something hasn't happened. The verb is in the perfect:

  Je ne l'ai pas vu **depuis** une   *I haven't seen him for a week.*
  semaine.

- to express how long something had been going on when something else happened:

| On était partis **depuis** à peine dix minutes qu'il s'est mis à pleuvoir des cordes. | *We had been gone just ten minutes when it started to rain cats and dogs.* |

■ **28.5.2 Pendant** is used when talking about a past event that is completed, or a future event. It is, however, often left out:

| J'ai habité **pendant** 5 ans à New York./J'ai habité 5 ans à New York. | *I lived in New York for five years.* |
| Nous serons à Paris **pendant** une semaine. | *We will be in Paris for a week.* |

■ **28.5.3 Il y a** means *ago*, except when followed by **que**:

| Ils sont partis **il y a** une heure. | *They left one hour ago.* |
| **Il y a** une heure que j'attends. | *I have been waiting for an hour.* |

This can also be expressed as:

J'attends depuis une heure.   *or*
Cela fait une heure que j'attends.

28.6 *Chez*

The preposition **chez** is used to mean:

- *at* or *to* someone's place:

| Je serai **chez** moi. | *I'll be at home.* |
| Je vais **chez** le docteur. | *I am going to the doctor's.* |

- staying *with* someone:

| Nous étions **chez** des amis. | *We stayed with friends.* |

- *in* or *to* someone's country:

  Il y a beaucoup de
  chômage **chez** vous?

  *Is there a lot of unemployment
  in your country?*

- *in* or *to* a company:

  Il y a eu des réductions
  d'effectifs **chez** Dumas S.A.

  *They have reduced the number
  of staff at Dumas.*

- *among* a group of people or animals:

  Le taux de suicide est plus
  élevé **chez** les jeunes.

  *The suicide rate is higher
  among young people.*

- *in* a person:

  Ce que j'aime **chez** elle,
  c'est sa franchise.

  *What I like in her is her
  frankness.*

- *in* someone's work:

  chez Molière

  in Molière's work

28.7 *Sur*

Sur means *on*:

  Pose-le **sur** la table.
  Put it on the table.

  C'est **sur** votre droite.
  It is on your right.

Though:

  La chambre donne **sur**
  la rue.
  The room overlooks the street.

In most cases **sur** means *on the top of*. Compare:

  sur le train
  on top of the train

  dans le train
  in/on the train

  sur la télé
  on the television set

  à la télé
  *on television
  (i.e., a program)*

29 The Present Tense

The present tense is used when talking about the present or habitual actions. Most verbs form their present tense by adding regular endings to their stem. For some of these verbs, irregularities occur within the stem while a few other verbs are altogether irregular.

29.1 Verbs Ending in *-er*

All verbs whose infinitive ends in **-er** have regular endings, except **aller** (*to go*) (see 29.3.2). Their present tense is formed by adding the appropriate endings to the stem, i.e., to the infinitive form without the **-er** ending:

	Endings	**parler** (*to speak*)	**acheter** (*to buy*)
je/j'	-e	parle	achète
tu	-es	parles	achètes
il/elle/on	-e	parle	achète
nous	-ons	parlons	achetons
vous	-ez	parlez	achetez
ils/elles	-ent	parlent	achètent

■ **29.1.1 Verbs Ending in *-e/-é* + consonant + *-er***
Most verbs ending in **e** + consonant + **er** follow the same pattern as **acheter** (see table above): the **-e/-é** changes to -è before a silent -e (e.g., in **j'achète** the last -e is not spoken, it is called a silent -e). A few other examples are:

achever	(*to complete*)	j'achève
geler	(*to freeze*)	je gèle
lever	(*to raise*)	je lève
peser	(*to weigh*)	je pèse
se promener	(*to go for a walk*)	je me promène

compléter	(to complete)	je complète
libérer	(to free)	je libère
posséder	(to own)	je possède
préférer	(to prefer)	je préfère
espérer	(to hope)	j'espère

- A few verbs ending in -eler or -eter double their consonant before a silent e like appeler (to call):

j'appelle	nous appelons
tu appelles	vous appelez
il/elle/on appelle	ils appellent

The most common ones are:

jeter	(to throw)	je jette
épeler	(to spell)	j'épelle
renouveler	(to renew)	je renouvelle

■ 29.1.2 Verbs Ending in -yer

In verbs ending in -oyer and -uyer the y changes to i in all but the nous and vous forms (i.e., before a silent e) while for verbs ending in -ayer, the change from y to i is optional:

| envoyer | (to send) | j'envoie, nous envoyons |
| payer | (to pay) | je paie/paye, nous payons |

■ 29.1.3 Verbs Ending in -cer and -ger

Verbs whose infinitive ends in -cer require a cedilla in the nous form to preserve the sound [s] since a c followed by a, o, or u is pronounced [k] (see 2.1.5): j'avance (I advance) but nous avançons (we advance).

Verbs whose infinitive ends in -ger require an -e after the -g in the nous form to preserve the sound [je]: nous nageons (we swim).

29.2 Verbs Ending in *-ir*

A number of verbs ending in **-ir**, like **finir** (*to finish*), **choisir** (*to choose*), and **remplir** (*to fill*) add -ss- before their plural endings:

	Endings	**finir**
je/j'	-s	finis
tu	-s	finis
il/elle/on	-t	finit
nous	-ssons	**finissons**
vous	-ssez	**finissez**
ils/elles	-ssent	**finissent**

Some verbs ending in **-ir** have, however, irregular present forms (see the verb tables, 52, for whole conjugations). Note that:

- verbs like **dormir** (*to sleep*), **partir** (*to leave*), **servir** (*to serve*), etc. have a shorter form in the singular: **je dors, nous dormons**

- verbs like **ouvrir** (*to open*), **offrir** (*to offer*), **souffrir** (*to suffer*), etc. have the singular endings of **-er** verbs: **j'ouvre**

- **tenir** (*to hold*), **venir** (*to come*), and their compound verbs (**obtenir**, *to obtain*; **devenir**, *to become*), etc. are very irregular: **je viens, je tiens**

29.3 Irregular Verbs

■ **29.3.1** Most verbs whose infinitive ends in **-re** and **-oir** have regular endings, but irregularities often occur within their stems (see examples in the table below). Note that verbs whose stem ends in -d or -t like **prendre** do not add any ending to their stem in the third person singular:

	Endings	**boire**	Endings	**prendre**
je/j'	-s	bois	-s	prends
tu	-s	bois	-s	prends
il/elle/on	-t	boit	-	prend
nous	-ons	**buvons**	-ons	**prenons**
vous	-ez	**buvez**	-ez	**prenez**
ils/elles/on	-ent	**boivent**	-ent	**prennent**

Many verbs' plural stems are different from their singular stems:

- **Conduire** (*to drive*) and most verbs ending in -uire, -aire (**plaire**, *to please*; **taire**, *to be quiet*), or -ire (**lire**, *to read*; **suffire**, *to be enough*) have a plural stem ending in -s: **je conduis, nous** *conduisons*; **je lis, nous** *lisons*. An exception is **j'écris, nous** *écrivons*.

- **Connaître** and other verbs ending in -aître have a plural stem ending in -ss: **je connais, nous** *connaissons*.

- **Peindre** and all verbs ending in -indre have a plural stem ending in -gn: **je peins, nous** *peignons*.

Other verbs do not follow a particular pattern and must be learned individually (see verb tables, 52).

■ **29.3.2** Modal verbs, **aller** (*to go*), **faire** (*to do, make*), **dire** (*to say*), **avoir** (*to have*), and **être** (*to be*) are particularly irregular (**dire, faire,** and **être** are the only verbs that do not have an -ez ending in the **vous** form!):

	dire	faire	être	avoir	aller
je/j'	dis	fais	**suis**	ai	vais
tu	dis	fais	es	as	vas
il/elle/on	dit	fait	est	a	va
nous	**disons**	faisons	**sommes**	avons	allons
vous	**dites**	**faites**	**êtes**	avez	allez
ils/elles	**disent**	font	sont	ont	vont

	devoir (*to owe, have to*)	pouvoir (*to be able to*)	vouloir (*to want to*)	savoir (*to know*)
je/j'	**dois**	**peux**	veux	sais
tu	**dois**	**peux**	veux	sais
il/elle/on	**doit**	**peut**	veut	sait
nous	devons	pouvons	voulons	savons
vous	devez	pouvez	voulez	savez
ils/elles	**doivent**	**peuvent**	**veulent**	savent

29.4 Use of the Present Tense

■ **29.4.1** The present tense is used to describe a current or usual situation, and to say what is happening now.

Nous allons à Seattle une   *We go to Seattle once a*
fois par mois.   *month.*

Depending on the context, **je travaille** can mean *I work* or *I am working*. There is no present continuous (i.e., like *I am doing*) in French. When it is important to stress that something *is* happening, use **être en train de** + the infinitive of the verb. For example:

Ne me dérangez pas!   *Do not disturb me!*
Je suis en train de travailler.   *I am working.*

■ **29.4.2** It is quite common to use the present tense when referring to the future:

L'année prochaine, je vais à la France.	*Next year, I am going to France.*

Note also that, when the main clause is in the future, the present is used after **si** instead of the future. The future is used after **quand** and **lorsque**:

S'il **fait** beau, on **ira** pique-niquer.	*If the weather is good, we'll go and have a picnic.*
Je lui en **parlerai** quand j'en **aurai** l'occasion.	*I will talk to him about it when I have the opportunity.*

■ **29.4.3** The present tense is used when talking about an action that started in the past and is still going on:

J'**habite** ici depuis deux ans.	*I have been living here for two years.*

■ **29.4.4** It is also used when saying that something has just happened. Use the present tense of **venir** + **de** + the infinitive of the verb:

Elle vient de partir.	*She has just left.*

■ **29.4.5** When recounting historical facts or a story in the past, the present tense can be used to make the event more immediate or dramatic:

À l'aéroport, tout paraissait normal. Soudain, ils **remarquent** que l'avion AB 256 **est** en train de faire demi-tour.	*At the airport, everything seemed normal. Suddenly they noticed that plane AB 256 was turning back.*
En 1962, les accords d'Evian **mettent** fin à une guerre qui **fit** plus de 2 000 000 morts.	*In 1962 the Evian agreement ended a war that caused more than 2 million deaths.*

30 The *Passé Composé* Tense

The **passé composé** is the most used tense when referring to the past. It is a compound tense: it consists of the present of **avoir** or of **être** followed by a past participle. (Words like **fait**, *done* and **allé**, *gone* are past participles. See 40.2 for past participle forms.)

30.1 The *Passé Composé* Tense Formed with *Avoir*

Most verbs build their **passé composé** tense with **avoir**. For example:

Tu **as lu** le journal?	*Have you read the paper?*
Nous **avons pris** le café sur la terrasse.	*We had coffee on the patio.*
Ils nous **ont offert** des chocolats.	*They gave us some chocolates.*

30.2 The *Passé Composé* Tense Formed with *Être*

The following verbs form their **passé composé** tense with **être**:

- reflexive verbs:
  Je me **suis couché** tard.   *I went to bed late.*

- a small group of other verbs:

aller	**je suis allé(e)**	*I went*
arriver	**je suis arrivé(e)**	*I arrived*
devenir	**je suis devenu(e)**	*I became*
entrer	**je suis entré(e)**	*I entered*
mourir	**il est mort**	*he died*
naître	**je suis né(e)**	*I was born*
partir	**je suis parti(e)**	*I left*
parvenir	**je suis parvenu(e)**	*I reached*
rentrer	**je suis rentré(e)**	*I went back in*

rester	**je suis resté(e)**	*I remained*
sortir	**je suis sorti(e)**	*I left*
tomber	**je suis tombé(e)**	*I fell*
venir	**je suis venu(e)**	*I came*

All these verbs, except **rester**, describe either a change in position (**aller, arriver, partir**) or a change of state (**naître, mourir**). They are all intransitive, i.e., they cannot have a direct object.

- A few verbs form their **passé composé** tense either with **avoir** or with **être** depending on whether they are used with a direct object or not. Compare:

	No direct object— **être** + past participle	Direct object— **avoir** + past participle
descendre	Je **suis descendu(e)**. *I went downstairs.*	J'**ai descendu** les escaliers. *I went down the stairs.*
monter	Je **suis monté(e)** sur le toit. *I climbed onto the roof.*	Je l'**ai monté** dans ma chambre. *I took it up to my room.*
passer	Je **suis passé(e)**. *I called in.*	Je l'**ai passé** à mon frère. *I passed it on to my brother.*
rentrer	Je **suis rentré(e)** à 5 h. *I came home at 5 pm.*	J'**ai rentré** la chaise. *I took the chair in.*
retourner	J'y **suis retourné(e)**. *I went back there.*	J'**ai retourné** la photo. *I turned the picture over.*
sortir	Je **suis sorti(e)** hier soir. *I went out last night.*	J'**ai sorti** le chien. *I took the dog out.*

30.3 The Agreement of Past Participles

The past participles of reflexive verbs and of verbs building their **passé composé** with **avoir** do not agree with the subject of the verb. However, they do for verbs building their **passé composé** with **être**. Note that the following rules apply not only to the **passé composé** but to all compound tenses (see 32, 34, 36, 38).

■ 30.3.1 Agreement for Verbs Taking *Avoir*

When the **passé composé** is formed with **avoir**, the past participle only agrees with a preceding direct object. So there is **no agreement** when the direct object comes **after** the verb:

J'ai **acheté une nouvelle voiture**.	*I have bought a new car.*
J'ai **envoyé la lettre** en recommandé.	*I sent the letter by registered mail.*

But there is **agreement** when the direct object comes **before** the verb:

J'aime ta nouvelle voiture. Tu **l'**as **payée** cher?	*I like your new car. Was it expensive?*
Ils n'ont pas encore reçu **la lettre que** je leur ai **envoyée** il y a trois jours.	*They still haven't received the letter I sent them three days ago.*

■ 30.3.2 Agreement for Reflexive Verbs

The past participle of a reflexive verb also agrees only with the preceding direct object. In most cases, the reflexive pronoun is a direct object:

Elles se sont promenées au bord de la rivière.	*They walked along the river.*

In some cases, however, the reflexive pronoun is an indirect object and there is no agreement. This is the case:

- when a part of the body is mentioned. Compare:

Elle s'est **lavée**.	*She washed (herself).*
Elle s'est **lavé les mains**.	*She washed her hands.*
Elle s'est **coupée**.	*She cut herself.*
Elle s'est **coupé le doigt**.	*She cut her finger.*

- with verbs like **dire à** (*to tell*), **écrire à** (*to write to*), and **téléphoner à** (*to telephone*) (*See 48.2.1 for a list.*)—the reflexive pronoun is used to mean *to each other*.

Ils se sont écrit de longues lettres.	*They wrote long letters to each other.*

■ 30.3.3 Agreement with *Être*

When the **passé composé** is formed with **être**, the past participle agrees, like an adjective, with the subject:

Ils sont **allés** au Japon.	*They went to Japan.*

30.4 Use of the *Passé Composé* Tense

The **passé composé** is used to describe completed actions or events that occurred once or several times in the past but not regularly.

Hier matin, **je suis allé** en ville et **j'ai fait** quelques courses.	*Yesterday morning, I went into town and did some shopping.*
J'ai vu ce film plusieurs fois.	*I have seen this film several times.*

The **passé composé** is also normally used when talking about what the weather was like at a specific time in the past:

Il a beaucoup **plu** la semaine dernière.	*It rained a lot last week.*

(See 31.3 for a description of when to use the **passé composé** and when to use the imperfect.)

The Imperfect Tense

The imperfect is used for descriptions and for habitual or continuous actions in the past.

31.1 Forms of the Imperfect Tense

The imperfect tense is formed by taking the **nous** form of the present tense, removing the **-ons** ending and replacing it with the following endings:

je	-ais	nous	-ions
tu	-ais	vous	-iez
il/elle/on	-ait	ils/elles	-aient

For example:

infinitive	present **nous** form	stem	imperfect
faire (*to do, make*)	nous faisons	fais-	je **faisais**
choisir (*to choose*)	nous choisissons	choisiss-	je **choisissais**

The only exception is **être: j'étais, tu étais, il était, nous étions, vous étiez, ils étaient.**

31.2 Use of the Imperfect Tense

While the **passé composé** is used for individual past actions or events, the imperfect is used for description and for habitual or continuous actions.

■ 31.2.1 For Description

The imperfect is used to describe people, things, or states of mind in the past:

La dernière fois que je l'ai vu, *Last time I saw him* (past event, **il avait** l'air en bonne forme. **passé composé**), *he looked well* (description, imperfect).

C'était bien?	*Was it good?*
Ce jour-là, **j'étais** de très mauvaise humeur.	*I was in a very bad mood on that day.*

Note the use of **il y avait** (*there was/were*) for descriptions:

    Il y avait beaucoup de monde.   *It was very crowded/busy.*

■ 31.2.2 For Habitual Action

The imperfect is also used to describe what people *used to* do or what *used to* happen in the past. Beware that no translation of *used to* is needed—nor available!—in French.

Quand j'étais étudiant, **j'allais** très souvent au cinéma.	*When I was a student, I used to go to the movies a lot.*

■ 31.2.3 For Continuous Action

The imperfect is also used to describe continuous actions, i.e., what *was* happening:

Je lisais tranquillement le journal quand on a sonné à la porte.	*I was peacefully reading the paper when someone rang the doorbell.*
Quand je suis descendu du train, **il pleuvait**.	*It was raining when I got off the train.*

The imperfect can be used with **depuis**:

Je travaillais chez IBM depuis trois ans quand j'ai décidé de changer de carrière.	*I had been working at IBM for three years when I decided to change careers.*

Aller and **venir de** are used in the imperfect followed by an infinitive to express that something *was going to happen* or *had just happened*:

J'allais le faire quand ils m'ont dit que ce n'était pas la peine.	*I was going to do it when they told me it was not necessary.*

Tu venais juste **de** sortir quand ils ont appelé.

You had just gone out when they called.

31.3 Imperfect or *Passé Composé*?

As a general rule:

- the **passé composé** is used for completed actions or events that happened once or a few times in the past

- the imperfect is used for actions or events that happened regularly in the past, for continuous actions, and for descriptions

Verbs like **penser** (*to think*) and **croire** (*to believe*) are more often used in the imperfect than in the **passé composé**: the **passé composé** is used when the thought or belief happened at a specific time in the past, while the imperfect is used to describe the state of mind during a longer period of time. Compare:

General thought—imperfect	Thought occurred at a specific time—**passé composé**
Je **pensais** qu'il n'y arriverait jamais. *I thought he would never get there.* Je **croyais** qu'elle était française. *I thought she was French.* Je **croyais** bien faire. *I thought it was the right thing to do.* (general belief)	J'**ai pensé** à vous hier. *I thought of you yesterday.* Tu **as pensé** à apporter ton agenda? *Did you remember to bring your diary?* J'**ai cru** bien faire. *I thought it was the right thing to do.* (what the person thought at the time)

When you talk about what the weather was like at a specific time in the past (last weekend, last holiday, etc.), it is more common to use the **passé composé**:

Samedi il a plu mais dimanche il a fait très beau.	*It rained on Saturday but on Sunday it was very nice.*

Note however that it is much more common to use **il y avait** when describing the weather; **il y a eu** is only used for something that happened suddenly or did not last long (such as a gust of wind, thunderstorm, etc.):

Il y avait beaucoup de brouillard.	*It was foggy.*
Dimanche, il a fait très chaud et vers six heures, **il y a eu** un gros orage.	*It was very hot on Sunday and at around six o'clock there was a big thunderstorm.*

32 The Pluperfect Tense

The pluperfect tense expresses what *had* happened or how a situation *had* been at a specific time in the past.

32.1 Forms of the Pluperfect Tense

The pluperfect tense is formed with an imperfect form of **avoir** or **être** and the past participle:

parler	**j'avais parlé**	*I had spoken*
rester	**j'étais resté(e)**	*I had remained*
se lever	**je m'étais levé(e)**	*I had got up*

The same verbs that take **être** in the **passé composé** take it in the pluperfect. All others take **avoir**. The rules for agreement are the same.

32.2 Use of the Pluperfect Tense

The pluperfect is used for an action or a fact that took place before another past event:

J'étais énervée parce qu'il n'avait rien préparé.	*I was annoyed because he hadn't prepared anything.*
Il y avait moins de monde que je ne l'avais craint.	*It was less busy than I had feared.*
J'avais presque terminé mon travail quand ils sont arrivés.	*I had nearly finished my work when they arrived.*
Ils étaient déjà partis quand leur père a téléphoné.	*They had already gone when their father called.*

33 The *Passé Simple* Tense

The **passé simple**, although hardly used any more in speech, is still used in formal written French (in newspaper articles, novels, children's books, etc.).

33.1 Forms of the *Passé Simple* Tense

Most verbs follow regular patterns in the **passé simple** tense. There are three types of possible endings:

	Verbs in -**er**	Most verbs in -**ir**, and some verbs in -**re** or -**oir**	Other possible endings
je/j'	-**ai**	-**is**	-**us**
tu	-**as**	-**is**	-**us**
il/elle/on	-**a**	-**it**	-**ut**
nous	-**âmes**	-**îmes**	-**ûmes**
vous	-**âtes**	-**îtes**	-**ûtes**
ils/elles	-**èrent**	-**irent**	-**urent**

Il entra précipitamment dans le salon. — *He rushed into the living room.*

Ils choisirent finalement la pièce la plus chère. — *They finally chose the most expensive piece.*

Note the forms of **avoir, être, faire,** and **venir**:

avoir: **j'eus**	être: **je fus**	faire: **je fis**	venir: **je vins**

Elle fut directrice de l'école pendant cinq ans. — *She was the school's principal for five years.*

Il fit un grand voyage. — *He went on a long trip.*

33.2 Use of the *Passé Simple* Tense

The **passé simple** is used, like the **passé composé**, to describe single, completed actions in the past. While the **passé composé** is used for most accounts of events or actions, the **passé simple** tends to be used for story telling. It appears:

- in newspaper articles when the article is recounting a story rather than being factual:

  Tout d'abord, nos instruments de prise de vue n'**attirèrent** pas l'attention.
  At first our camera equipment didn't attract anyone's attention.

- in novels, poems, stories, and children's stories:

  Un jour, un loup qui passait par là **frappa** à la porte de la maisonnette.
  One day, a wolf, who was passing by, knocked on the door of the small house.

  (Note that it is used together with the imperfect in the same way as the **passé composé** is used.)

- for historical accounts:

  La guerre **fit** des millions de morts.
  The war caused millions of deaths.

It is rarely used in letter writing, even in formal letters. It is also rarely used in spoken French, except for the verbs **être** and **avoir**. The **nous** and **vous** forms sound archaic and are used even less frequently than the other forms.

34 The Preterite Perfect Tense

The preterite perfect tense is a compound tense. It is used in careful French in conjunction with the **passé simple**.

34.1 Forms of the Preterite Perfect Tense

The preterite perfect is formed with the **passé simple** of **avoir** or **être** and the past participle:

parler	**j'eus parlé**	*I had spoken*
rester	**je fus resté(e)**	*I had remained*
se lever	**je me fus levé(e)**	*I had got up*

All the verbs that form their **passé composé** tense with **être** also form their preterite perfect tense with **être** (see 30.2).

The agreement rules for the past participle are the same as in the **passé composé** tense (see 30.3).

34.2 Use of the Preterite Perfect Tense

The preterite perfect is a literary tense. It expresses the fact that the action or event happened before one described in the **passé simple**. It is used mainly after **quand** (*when*), **lorsque** (*when*), **aussitôt que** (*as soon as*), **dès que** (*as soon as*), **après que** (*after*), and **à peine que** (*hardly, scarcely*):

A peine eut-il terminé que des larmes lui montèrent aux yeux.   *He had hardly finished when tears came to his eyes.*

35 | The Future Tense

35.1 Forms of the Future Tense

All verbs—regular and irregular—take the same endings in the future tense: **-ai, -as, -a, -ons, -ez,** and **-ont** (the endings of the present tense of **avoir**).

■ **35.1.1** Most verbs add these endings to their infinitive form, though **-re** verbs drop the **-e** from the infinitive:

	parler (to speak)	**choisir** (to choose)	**prendre** (to take)
je	parlerai	choisirai	prendrai
tu	parleras	choisiras	prendras
il/elle/on	parlera	choisira	prendra
nous	parlerons	choisirons	prendrons
vous	parlerez	choisirez	prendrez
ils/elles	parleront	choisiront	prendront

Verbs ending in **-e** + consonant + **-er** double the consonant or have a grave accent in the future as they do in the present singular (see 29.1.1):

| appeler | **j'appellerai** | *I will call* |
| acheter | **j'achèterai** | *I will buy* |

Verbs ending **-é** + consonant + **-er** traditionally keep the **-é** in the future. Nowadays, however, because the pronunciation has changed (the **-é** is now pronounced more or less like an **-è**) both spellings are found: **j'espérerai/j'espèrerai** (*I will hope*), **je compléterai/je complèterai** (*I will complete*), etc.

■ **35.1.2** A number of verbs do not use their infinitive as a stem although they do use the regular endings. The most common are:

aller	j'irai	I will go
avoir	j'aurai	I will have
courir	je courrai	I will run
devoir	je devrai	I will have to/owe
envoyer	j'enverrai	I will send
être	je serai	I will be
faire	je ferai	I will do/make
il faut	il faudra	it will be necessary
mourir	je mourrai	I will die
pouvoir	je pourrai	I will be able
il pleut	il pleuvra	it will rain
recevoir	je recevrai	I will receive
savoir	je saurai	I will know
tenir	je tiendrai	I will hold
valoir	je vaudrai	I will be worth
venir	je viendrai	I will come
voir	je verrai	I will see
vouloir	je voudrai	I will want

35.2 Use of the Future Tense

The future tense is used to refer to the future:

J'irai les voir demain.	I will go and see them tomorrow.

The future tense cannot be used after **si**—except when **si** is used to mean *whether*:

S'il fait beau, on ira se promener.	If the weather is good, we'll go for a walk.
Je me demande s'il viendra.	I wonder whether he will come.

It can be used after **quand** (*when*), **lorsque** (*when*), **aussitôt que** (*as soon as*), **dès que** (*as soon as*), **pendant que** (*while*), and **tant que** (*while*):

Nous leur en parlerons **quand ils viendront.**	We'll talk about it when they come.

Like the present (see 29.4.5), it can be used in a piece of literature or a newspaper article referring to a past event to give more immediacy to the narrative or to emphasize particular events:

En 1974, les mouvements écologistes décident de présenter un candidat aux élections présidentielles. Dumont n'**obtiendra** certes que 1,32% des voix, mais l'écologie politique est née.	*In 1974, the ecology movement decided to run a candidate in the (French) presidential elections. Dumont obtained only 1.32% of the votes, but political ecology was born.*

35.3 Other Ways to Express the Future

■ **35.3.1** The present is often used for future actions—but not for future states of mind or states of affairs:

Dans un mois, je vais à Miami.	*I'll go to Miami next month.*
Nous serons très heureux de vous revoir	*We'll be very pleased to see you again.*

■ **35.3.2** The present tense of the verb **aller** followed by an infinitive is used to express that something *is going* to happen:

Je vais aller chez ma sœur.	*I am going to go to my sister's.*

36 The Future Perfect Tense

The future perfect tense is a compound tense. It is used more often in French than in English.

36.1 Forms of the Future Perfect Tense

The future perfect is formed by using a future form of **avoir** or **être** and a past participle:

j'aurai fait	*I will have done*
je serai parti	*I will have gone*

The verbs that form their **passé composé** tense with **être**, also form their future perfect tense with **être** (see 30.2). The rules for agreement of the past participle are the same as in the **passé composé** (see 30.3).

36.2 Use of the Future Perfect Tense

It is used to express what *will have* happened by a given time in the future:

Nous aurons terminé d'ici demain.	*We will have finished by tomorrow.*

It is mostly used after **quand** and other conjunctions of time in situations where English would use the perfect tense:

Tu pourras regarder la télé lorsque **tu auras fini** tes devoirs.	*You can watch television when you have finished your homework.*

37 The Present Conditional Tense

The conditional is used to express what, under certain conditions, *would* happen or be (present conditional) or what *would have* happened or been (past conditional, see 38).

37.1 Forms of the Present Conditional Tense

The present conditional forms are very close to the future forms. They have the same stems as the future tense (i.e., the infinitive for regular verbs) and use the imperfect endings -ais, -ais, -ait, -ions, -iez, -aient:

	parler (*to speak*)	**choisir** (*to choose*)	**prendre** (*to take*)
je	parlerais	choisirais	prendrais
tu	parlerais	choisirais	prendrais
il/elle/on	parlerait	choisirait	prendrait
nous	parlerions	choisirions	prendrions
vous	parleriez	choisiriez	prendriez
ils/elles	parleraient	choisiraient	prendraient

The same irregularities that occur in the future also occur in the present conditional (see 35.1.2):

appeler	**j'appellerais**	*I would call*
acheter	**j'achéterais**	*I would buy*
aller	**j'irais**	*I would go*
avoir	**j'aurais**	*I would have*
courir	**je courrais**	*I would run*
devoir	**je devrais**	*I would have to/owe*
envoyer	**j'enverrais**	*I would send*
être	**je serais**	*I would be*
faire	**je ferais**	*I would do/make*

il faut	**il faudrait**	*it would be necessary*
mourir	**je mourrais**	*I would die*
pouvoir	**je pourrais**	*I would be able*
il pleut	**il pleuvrait**	*it would rain*
recevoir	**je recevrais**	*I would receive*
savoir	**je saurais**	*I would know*
tenir	**je tiendrais**	*I would hold*
valoir	**je vaudrais**	*it would be worth*
venir	**je viendrais**	*I would come*
voir	**je verrais**	*I would see*
vouloir	**je voudrais**	*I would like*

37.2 Use of the Present Conditional Tense

The conditional present is used:

- to express what *would* happen or what someone *would* do in certain conditions:

  Je le **ferais** avec plaisir s'ils me le demandaient.   *I would gladly do it if they asked me to.*

  Note that the verb after **si** is in the imperfect, not in the conditional.

- to express a preference, a need, a wish, or a polite request:

  Je préférerais le rouge.   *I'd prefer the red one.*

  Il me **faudrait** un kilo de farine.   *I'll need a kilo (about two pounds) of flour.*

  Je voudrais trois croissants, s'il vous plaît.   *I would like three croissants, please.*

  Je vous **serais** reconnaissant de me faire parvenir votre tarif.   *I'd be grateful if you could send me your price list.*

- to give advice:

  Vous devriez vous dépêcher!   *You should hurry up!*

  A votre place, **je** ne **m'inquiéterais** pas.   *I would not worry if I were you.*

- to express a possibility:
  Il y aurait peut-être une   *There might be a better*
  meilleure solution!   *solution!*

  Note also the use of **on dirait que**… to mean *it looks as if*:
  On dirait qu'il va pleuvoir.   *It looks as if it is going to rain.*

- to express noncommitment about the accuracy of a
  statement:
  Un carambolage s'est   *An accident has occured on*
  produit sur l'autoroute.   *the highway. Several people*
  Il y aurait plusieurs blessés   *are said to be injured.*
  graves.

- in reported speech:
  Je lui ai dit qu'**il ferait**   *I told him he would do better*
  mieux de partir.   *to leave.*

38 The Past Conditional Tense

The past conditional tense is mainly used to express what *would have* happened if certain circumstances had been met.

38.1 Forms of the Past Conditional Tense

The past conditional is formed with a conditional form of **avoir** or **être** and the past participle:

On aurait mieux **fait** de ne rien dire.	*We shouldn't have said anything.*
Sans son casque, **elle** se **serait** gravement **blessée.**	*Without her helmet she would have been seriously injured.*

38.2 Use of the Past Conditional Tense

It is mainly used:

* to express what someone *would*, *should*, or *could have* done or what *would*, *should*, or *could have* happened in certain circumstances. Note the use of the pluperfect after **si**:

Ils seraient restés s'ils avaient trouvé à se loger.	*They would have stayed if they had found a hotel room.*
J'aurais dû les prévenir.	*I should have warned them.*
Tu aurais pu l'aider!	*You could have helped her!*

* to express what someone *would have* liked to do. It is often accompanied by **bien**:

J'aurais bien aimé être là!	*I would have liked to have been there.*

39 The Infinitive

The infinitive is the basic form of the verb, for example, **aimer** (*to like*), **être** (*to be*), etc. It is the form in which verbs are listed in dictionaries.

39.1 Forms of the Infinitive

■ **39.1.1** The infinitive ends in **-er, -ir, -re,** or **-oir: habiter** (*to live*), **finir** (to finish), **faire** (*to do, make*), **pleuvoir** (*to rain*).

■ **39.1.2** When referring to a past action, the past infinitive must be used. It is simply formed by using **avoir** or **être** and the past participle of the verb:

Après **avoir appris** la nouvelle, nous sommes tout de suite allés la voir.	*After hearing/having heard the news, we went to see her immediately.*

■ **39.1.3** When negated, the two parts of the negation come before the infinitive:

Il a décidé de **ne pas continuer** ses études.	*He has decided not to continue his studies.*

39.2 Use of the Infinitive

It is used:

- in instructions such as those found in recipes or signs:

Ajouter 250 grammes de farine.	*Add 250 g. (about 1¾ cups) flour.*

- as the subject of a sentence, like a noun:

Elever des enfants n'est pas facile.	*Bringing up children is not easy.*

- after certain prepositions, for example:

avant de	*before*
après	*after* (use a past infinitive)
au lieu de	*instead of*
comment	*how*
pour/afin de	*to/in order to*
sans	*without*
Il est parti **sans m'avoir** donné la clef.	*He has gone without giving me the key.*

- after a verb plus noun combination, e.g., **avoir envie de...** (*to feel like . . .*)—(see 48.3)—or an adjective (see 13.2/3):

  Il est difficile **de faire** mieux. *It's difficult to do better.*

- after a verb (see 48):

J'aime **marcher**.	*I like walking.*
Il me demande **de partir**.	*He is asking me to leave.*
Je continue **à travailler**.	*I continue to work.*

- in questions and exclamations:

Que **faire**?	*What shall I/we do?*

Note that after verbs of willing, likes, and expectation—**vouloir** (*to want*), **aimer** (*to like*), **préférer** (*to prefer*), etc.—an infinitive construction is not possible when the subject of the second verb is not also the subject of the first verb. **Que** + subjunctive is used instead (see 43.2):

Je veux le faire.	*I want to do it.*

but:

Je veux que **tu** le fasses.	*I want **you** to do it.*

40 Participles

There are two types of participles: the present participle, e.g., **souriant** (*smiling*), and the past participle, e.g., **terminé** (*finished*).

40.1 The Present Participle

The present participle of a French verb ends in -ant: **gagnant** (*winning*).

■ 40.1.1 Forming the Present Participle

It is formed by taking the **nous** form of the present tense and replacing the -**ons** ending by -**ant**:

| faire | nous faisons | **faisant** | *doing* |
| prendre | nous prenons | **prenant** | *taking* |

There are only three exceptions:

avoir	**ayant**	*having*
être	**étant**	*being*
savoir	**sachant**	*knowing*

■ 40.1.2 Uses of the Present Participle

The present participle can be used as an adjective or as a verb.

- As an adjective it agrees with the noun or pronoun it refers to:

  | Elles sont **accueillantes**. | *They are welcoming.* |
  | La semaine **suivante**, nous avons visité les châteaux de la Loire. | *The following week we visited the castles of the Loire valley.* |

- Used as a verb the present participle is used to describe a situation, an action, or to explain it:

  | Elle entra **portant** un plateau avec du café et des biscuits. | *She came in carrying a tray with coffee and cookies.* |

Etant intéressés par votre   *We are interested in your offer*
offre, nous avons le plaisir   *and would like to place an order.*
de passer une commande.

Used as a verb, the present participle is invariable. Like
other verb forms it can be followed by objects, preceded
by object pronouns and have negatives around it:

Ne le **voyant** pas venir,   *Seeing no sign of him, I started*
j'ai commencé toute seule.   *out on my own.*

The present participle is preceded by **en**:

• to emphasize that two actions happen(ed) at the same
  time:
  Il écoute la radio **en**   *He listens to the radio while*
  travaillant.   *working.*

• and/or to explain how something happens/happened:
  Elle s'est fait mal au dos   *She hurt her back falling off a*
  en tombant de cheval.   *horse.*

There are various ways of translating **en** + present
participle into English:

• *when/while/on* + present participle:
  Elle nous a souri **en**   *She smiled at us when/on*
  partant.   *leaving.*

• *when/while/as* + subject + verb:
  Elle s'est brûlée **en**   *She burned herself when/as she*
  touchant la poêle.   *touched the frying pan.*

• verb + preposition:
  Elle a traversé la rue **en**   *She ran across the street.*
  courant.

Tout can precede **en** + present participle. This either:

• emphasizes even more the simultaneity of two actions:
  Tout en faisant la cuisine,   *While doing the cooking, we*
  nous avons bien bavardé.   *had a good chat.*

- or expresses a contrast:

Tout en étant bons copains, nous ne partageons pas toujours les mêmes opinions.	*Although we are good friends, we don't always share the same opinions.*

■ 40.1.3 When Not to Use the Present Participle

In many cases an -**ing** form is used in English where a present participle cannot be used in French:

- in French the past participle, not the present participle, is used to describe postures (see 40.2.2).

- when the present participle is part of a continuous tense: there are no continuous tenses (e.g., *I am reading, I was working,* etc.) in French.

To translate the English present continous, the present tense is used in French:

Laisse-moi tranquille, je fais mes devoirs.	*Leave me alone. I am doing my homework.*

For the English past continuous, French uses the imperfect:

A l'époque, il travaillait chez Sears.	*At the time, he was working for Sears.*

- after certain verbs, an -**ing** form is often used in English (e.g., *to like/to enjoy doing,* etc.) where in French an infinitive is used (see 39.2):

Vous aimez travailler ici?	*Do you like working here?*

40.2 The Past Participle

The past participle is the verb form used with **avoir** or **être** in compound tenses (e.g., **j'ai fini**, *I finished*).

■ 40.2.1 Forming the Past Participle

Past participles usually have one of the following endings:

- **-é** All verbs whose infinitive ends in **-er** have their past participle ending in **-é**:

  travailler   j'ai **travaillé**   *I have worked/I worked*

- **-u** A number of verbs have their past participle ending in **-u**:

courir	**couru**	*run*
falloir	**fallu**	*had to*
perdre	**perdu**	*lost*
résoudre	**résolu**	*resolved*
tenir	**tenu**	*held*
vendre	**vendu**	*sold*
venir	**venu**	*come*
vivre	**vécu**	*lived*
vouloir	**voulu**	*wanted*

  Some of them have only one syllable:

boire	**bu**	*drunk*
croire	**cru**	*believed*
devoir	**dû**	*had to/owed*
lire	**lu**	*read*
plaire	**plu**	*pleased*
pleuvoir	**plu**	*rained*
pouvoir	**pu**	*able*
savoir	**su**	*known*
voir	**vu**	*seen*

  Note that verbs ending in **-aître** and **-cevoir** have a shortened past participle:

connaître	**connu**	*knew*
recevoir	**reçu**	*received*

- **-i** Most verbs whose infinitive ends in **-ir**, as well as **suffire** (*to be enough*) and **suivre** (*to follow*), have their past participle ending in **-i**:

  dormir   j'ai **dormi**   *I have slept/I slept*

- **-ert** Ouvrir (*to open*) and its compound verbs, e.g.,
  découvrir (*to discover*), **offrir** (*to offer*), and
  souffrir (*to suffer*) have their past participle ending
  in -**ert**:
  Qu'est-ce qu'il t'a **offert**? *What did he give you?*

Other past participles do not follow a particular
pattern. The most common ones are:

avoir	**eu**	*had*
être	**été**	*been*
faire	**fait**	*done, made*
conduire	**conduit**	*driven*
dire	**dit**	*said*
écrire	**écrit**	*written*
mettre	**mis**	*put*
prendre	**pris**	*taken*

■ **40.2.2 Uses of the Past Participle**
The past participle can be used as an adjective or a verb.
It is also used to form compound tenses and the passive.

- When the past participle is used as an adjective, it
  agrees with the noun or pronoun it refers to:
  Je voudrais ma viande *I'd like my meat well cooked.*
  bien **cuite**.

  Note that the past participle is used in French to
  describe postures (**allongé/couché**, *lying*; **assis**, *sitting*;
  etc.):
  Ils étaient **allongés** sur la *They were lying on the beach.*
  plage.

- When used as a verb the past participle agrees with the
  subject of the main clause:
  Prise de remords, elle *Stricken by remorse, she*
  avoua tout. *confessed everything.*

41 The Imperative

The imperative is used when expressing a command, an instruction, or a request.

41.1 Forms

The imperative has three forms. They correspond with the **tu**, **nous**, and **vous** forms of the present tense. The pronoun is left out:

tu form	Prends le train!	*Take the train!*
nous form	Prenons le train!	*Let's take the train!*
vous form	Prenez le train!	*Take the train!*

Note that:

* the -s of the **tu** form of -er verbs is dropped, except when **en** or **y** follow the verb:
  Travaille! *Work!*
  Parle plus lentement! *Speak more slowly!*
  Achètes-en deux paquets! *Buy two packages (of it).*

* **avoir** (*to have*), **être** (*to be*), **savoir** (*to know*), and **vouloir** (*to want*) are irregular:

avoir	être	savoir	vouloir
aie	sois	sache	(no form)
ayons	soyons	sachons	(no form)
ayez	soyez	sachez	veuillez

Veuillez vous asseoir. *Would you please sit down.*

41.2 The Imperative with Object Pronouns

■ **41.2.1** In positive commands, object pronouns come after the verb and are linked to it by an hyphen:
  Prends-le! *Take it!*

The imperative of reflexive verbs is built in the same way:

Réveille-toi!   *Wake up!*

When two object pronouns are used, the direct object pronouns come before the indirect object pronouns:

Prête-le-lui!   *Lend it to him/her!*

But **en** comes last:

Donne-m'en!   *Give me some!*

■ **41.2.2** In negative commands, the object pronouns come before the verb in the same order as they do in other tenses (see 23.3):

Ne lui dites rien!   *Don't tell him anything!*

Ne leur en parlez pas!   *Don't talk to them about it!*

42 The Passive

In the passive, the action is not defined in terms of who performs it, but rather in terms of whom or what the action affects. Compare:

Active—subject performing the action	Passive—subject not performing the action
Ils ont signé le contrat hier. *They signed the contract yesterday.*	Le contrat **a été signé** hier. *The contract **was signed** yesterday.*
Le chien a mordu Pierre. *The dog has bitten Pierre.*	Pierre **a été mordu** par le chien. *Pierre has been bitten by the dog.*

42.1 Forming the Passive

The passive is formed in the same way as in English: with the appropriate tense of **être** and the past participle. **Par** is used for *by*.

Les actualités **sont présentées par** M. Poivre d'Arvor. *The news is presented by Mr. Poivre d'Arvor.*

L'entretien **sera interprété par** Mme Bertin. *The interview will be interpreted by Madame Bertin.*

42.2 Use of the Passive

The passive is used a lot in journalistic or business French:

Le RMI **a été augmenté** de 1,5%. *The RMI (social security benefit) has been increased by 1.5 percent.*

La société **a été reprise** par DMC. *The company was taken over by DMC.*

The passive is, however, used a lot less in day-to-day spoken French than it is in English. Note that:

- **on** is often used instead of a passive construction:

  On a construit un nouveau pont. — *A new bridge has been built.*

- the fact that a passive construction is used in English does not mean that a passive construction is possible in French. Beware that in phrases like *I was given . . ., we were told . . ., he was asked . . ., they were offered . . .,* etc. a literal translation is impossible in French. In such cases, the French tends to use **on**. Compare:

  On m'a donné une semaine pour le faire. — *I was given a week to do it.*

  On nous a demandé de venir tout de suite. — *We were asked to come straight away.*

- in a few cases, a reflexive verb in French is used where English uses a passive form (see 45.1.4):

  Ce vin se boit frais. — *This wine is drunk chilled.*

43 The Subjunctive

All the tenses described in Sections 29 to 38 are in the indicative mood and this is the way you are most likely to encounter and use them. However, parallel to the indicative mood is the subjunctive mood, which also has a range of tenses (of which the present is by far the most commonly used). The difference between the indicative and the subjunctive moods is explained in 43.2.

43.1 Forms of the Present Subjunctive

■ **43.1.1** In the subjunctive *all* verbs except **avoir** and **être** use the same endings as present tense indicative -**er** verbs in their singular and **ils** forms:

je	-e		
tu	-es	ils/elles	-ent
il/elle/on	-e		

For most verbs, these endings are added to the same stem as they use in the **ils** form of the present tense indicative. -**er** verbs therefore have the same singular and **ils** forms in the present subjunctive and the present indicative:

	Present indicative	Stem	Present subjunctive
travailler (*to work*)	ils travaillent	travaill-	**je travaille**
appeler (*to call*)	ils appellent	appell-	**j'appelle**
prendre (*to take*)	ils prennent	prenn-	**je prenne**
finir (*to finish*)	ils finissent	finiss-	**je finisse**

■ **43.1.2** The **nous** and **vous** forms of nearly all verbs are the same in the subjunctive as in the imperfect indicative:

appeler	nous appelions, vous appeliez
prendre	nous prenions, vous preniez
finir	nous finissions, vous finissiez

■ **43.1.3** A few verbs do not follow the above pattern (see verb tables for whole conjugation):

avoir	j'aie	to have
être	je sois	to be
aller	j'aille	to go
faire	je fasse	to do, make
vouloir	je veuille	to want
pouvoir	je puisse	to be able

43.2 Use of the Present Subjunctive

The subjunctive is mainly used after verbs expressing an emotion, a wish, liking and disliking, a possiblility, an order or a doubt, and after some conjunctions when an infinitive construction is not possible, i.e., when the two verbs have different subjects. Compare:

| Je viens dimanche. | I'll come on Sunday. (indicative) |
| Je préfère venir dimanche. | I prefer to come on Sunday. (indicative—same subjects) |

but:

| Je préfère que **vous** veniez dimanche. | I prefer that **you** come on Sunday. (subjunctive—different subjects) |

■ **43.2.1** The main categories of verbs that are followed by **que** + the subjunctive when an infinitive construction is not possible are as follows:

• Verbs expressing emotion (**être content, désolé**, *to be happy, sorry*, etc.), fear (**avoir peur**, *to be afraid*, etc.), regret and wish (**souhaiter**, *to wish*; **désirer**, *to desire*—but not **espérer**, *to hope!*), willing (**vouloir**, *to want*; **demander**, *to ask*, etc.), likes and dislikes (**aimer**, *to like*; **préférer**, *to prefer*, etc.), and expectation (**attendre**, *to wait*, etc.):

Je veux le faire moi-même.	*I want to do it myself.*

but:

Je veux qu'il le fasse tout de suite.	*I want **him** to do it right away.*

- Verbs expressing a doubt (**douter**, *to doubt*), a possibility (**il est possible, probable que**, *it is possible, probable that*, etc.), denial (**nier**, *to deny*, etc.):

Je doute d'avoir tout vu.	*I doubt I have seen everything.*

but:

Je doute qu'ils aient tout vu.	*I doubt **they** have seen everything.*

- A number of impersonal constructions (**il est nécessaire**, *it is necessary*, **important**, *important*, **normal**, *natural*, **naturel**, *natural*, **dommage**, *shame*, **utile**, *useful*, **il vaut mieux**, *it is better*, etc.) are followed by **que** + the subjunctive when the second verb has a very specific subject; otherwise an infinitive construction is used:

Il est essentiel d'agir rapidement.	*It is essential to act quickly.*

but:

Il est essentiel que le comité agisse rapidement.	*It is essential for the committee to act quickly.*

- **Il faut** (*it is necessary*) is used both with an infinitive construction and with **que** and the subjunctive:

Il me faut aller à la banque.   *I must go to the bank.*
or Il faut que j'aille à la banque.

- A few verbs and verbal phrases express doubt or uncertainty only in the negative (**je ne suis pas sûr que**, *I am not sure that*; **je ne pense pas que**, *I don't think that*, etc.) and are therefore followed by the subjunctive only when used in the negative:
Je crois qu'il est malade.   *I think he is ill.*

but:
Je ne crois pas qu'il soit   *I don't think he is ill.*
malade.

■ **43.2.2** Some conjunctions are followed by the subjunctive, for example **bien que** (*although*), **jusqu'à ce que** (*until*), and **malgré que** (*despite that*), etc. (for list, see 49.2). Some conjunctions that take the subjunctive can also be used with an infinitive construction when both verbs have the same subject. They usually change slightly:

with infinitive	with subjunctive	
à condition de	à condition que	*provided that*
afin de/pour	afin que/pour que	*so that*
à moins de	à moins que	*unless*
avant de	avant que	*before*
sans	sans que	*without*

Appelle-la avant de partir.   *Call her quickly before you go.*
but:
Appelle-la avant qu'il   *Call her before it is too late!*
(ne) soit trop tard!

With **à moins que**, **avant que** and also **de peur/de crainte que** (*for fear that*), **ne** precedes the subjunctive form in careful French although it doesn't have a negative meaning.

De sorte que, de façon que, and **de manière que** (which all mean *so that*) are followed by the subjunctive when they express purpose rather than consequence (see 49.2).

■ **43.2.3 Subjunctive in Three Kinds of Relative Clauses**
The subjunctive is needed:

• after a superlative or adjectives like **premier** (*first*), **dernier** (*last*), and **seul** (*only*) followed by **qui** or **que**:

C'est le meilleur guide que je connaisse.   *He is the best guide I know of.*

C'est la seule chose qui compte.   *It is the only thing which matters.*

• after **personne** (*no one*) and **rien** (*nothing*) followed by **qui** or **que**, and after **quelqu'un qui/que** (*anyone who*) when used in a question:

Y a-t-il quelqu'un qui sache jouer de la guitare?   *Is there anyone who knows how to play the guitar?*

• to express the notion of looking for something or someone:

Je cherche un F4 qui soit central mais pas trop bruyant.   *I am looking for a three-bedroom apartment that is centrally located but relatively quiet.*

■ **43.2.4 Subjunctive as an Imperative**
The subjunctive is used for the imperative of **avoir, être, savoir**, and **vouloir** (see 41.1) and to express a command in the third person singular and plural:

Que personne ne sorte!   *Nobody is to go out!*

Qu'ils fassent attention!   *They must be careful!*

■ **43.2.5 Subjunctive After Certain Indefinite Expressions**
The subjunctive is needed after expressions like **quoi**

qui/que (*whatever*), quel que (*whatever*), qui que (*whoever*),
où que (*wherever*), which describe something indefinite:

Avez-vous besoin de quoi que ce soit?	*Do you need anything?*
Il aime les défis, quels qu'ils soient.	*He likes challenges, whatever they might be.*

43.3 Other Tenses of the Subjunctive

There are another three tenses of the subjunctive: the past
which is used frequently, and the imperfect and the
pluperfect which now sound archaic and are only met in
literature or very formal French.

■ 43.3.1 The Past Subjunctive

The past subjunctive is used when a **passé composé** would
be used if a subjunctive construction were not required. It
is formed with the present subjunctive of **avoir** or **être**
and the past participle:

Je suis désolé que **vous** n'**ayez** pas **pu** venir.	*I am sorry you were not able to come.*
Nous nous voyons très rarement bien que **nous soyons restés** de bons amis.	*We see each other very rarely although we have remained good friends.*

■ 43.3.2 The Imperfect Subjunctive

The imperfect subjunctive is very rarely used in
contemporary French. You may however encounter it in
literature. It is formed by adding the following endings to
the third person singular of the **passé simple**:

je	-sse	nous	-ssions
tu	-sses	vous	-ssiez
il/elle/on	-^t	ils/elles	-ssent

Il faudrait qu'**il** lui **parlât**.	*He ought to talk to him/her.*
Il vaudrait mieux qu'**il prît** le train.	*It would be better if he took the train.*

■ 43.3.3 The Pluperfect Subjunctive

The pluperfect subjunctive is rarely used anymore but you might encounter it in noncontemporary literature. It is used where nowadays a past conditional is preferred. It is formed with an imperfect subjunctive form of **avoir** or **être** and the past participle:

Il lui apprit que s'**il eût choisi** M. Castanède, **il eût** peut-être **agi** avec plus de prudence.	*He told him that were he to have chosen Mr. Castanède, he would have acted perhaps more wisely.*

(Stendhal, *Le Rouge et le Noir*)

44 Use of Modal Verbs and of *Être*

44.1 *Devoir*

Devoir (for its conjugation see verb tables, 52) means, in most cases, *must, have to*:

J'ai dû attendre une heure.	*I had to wait for an hour.*
Nous devrons louer une voiture.	*We'll have to rent a car.*
Elle doit avoir la quarantaine.	*She must be in her forties.*

It is, however, also the equivalent of *should, ought to, to be supposed to,* and *to be due to*:

Vous devriez rouler plus lentement.	*You should drive more slowly.*
Il aurait dû s'y prendre plus tôt.	*He should have done it earlier.*
Je devais y aller mais j'ai eu un empêchement de dernière minute.	*I was supposed/due to go there but, at the last minute, I was unable to.*

44.2 *Vouloir*

Vouloir (for its conjugation see verb tables, 52) means *to want, to wish,* and *to have the intention of*:

Je veux que tu y ailles.	*I want you to go there.*

(for **vouloir que** + subjunctive, see 43.2.1)

Elle veut passer une année au Canada.	*She wants/intends to spend a year in Canada.*

Note that when asking for something, it is not very polite to say **je veux**; the conditional form **je voudrais** is used instead. It is the equivalent of the English form *I would like*:

Je voudrais un café, s'il vous plaît.	*I'd like coffee, please.*

44.3 *Pouvoir*

■ **44.3.1** **Pouvoir** (for its conjugation see 29.3.2) is used to express possibility and ability (*can, to be able to*) and permission (*may*):

Il **pourrait** y avoir du verglas.	*There could be ice on the road.*
Je n'ai pas **pu** le faire.	*I was not able to do it.*
Je **peux** ouvrir la fenêtre?	*May I open the window?*

Note that **puis-je** is used in questions as the inverted form of **je peux**:

Puis-je fumer?	*May I smoke?*

In positive statements, *may* is normally expressed by **peut-être**:

Il a **peut-être** téléphoné pendant notre absence.	*He may have phoned while we were away.*

■ **44.3.2** When Not to Use *Pouvoir*

• With verbs of perception (e.g., **entendre**, *to hear*; **sentir**, *to feel/to smell*; **voir**, *to see*) and with **trouver** (*to find*), **pouvoir** is usually omitted:

Je ne le trouve pas.	*I can't find it.*

• **Pouvoir** cannot be used to express that you *can* do something because you have learned how to do it; **savoir** is the verb to use here. Compare:

On ne peut pas nager: l'eau est trop froide.	*We can't swim, the water is too cold.*
Elle sait nager?	*Can she swim? (Has she learned how to swim?)*

44.4 *Savoir* and *Connaître*

Savoir and **connaître** both mean *to know* but are not interchangeable. **Savoir** is used when referring to knowledge or skill and **connaître** when referring to acquaintance or to what people have come across:

Vous **savez** à quelle heure il vient?	*Do you know what time he is coming?*
Je ne **sais** pas.	*I don't know.*
Vous **connaissez** M. Desrosier?	*Do you know Mr. Desrosier?*
Tu **connais** ce livre?	*Do you know this book?*

44.5 *Falloir*

■ **44.5.1 Il faut** means *must* when used with:

- an infinitive, instead of **on doit, nous devons**:
  Il faut partir.   *We must go.*

- an indirect object pronoun + infinitive:
  Il lui faut partir.   *He/she must go.*

- **que** + subjunctive:
  Il faut que je parte.   *I must go.*

■ **44.5.2 Il faut** means *to need* or *to take* (to express how long something takes):

Il me faut un formulaire.	*I need a form.*
Il faut 4 heures.	*It takes four hours.*

44.6 "To be" is Not Always *Être*

There are a few cases where *to be* is not translated by **être** in French.

■ **44.6.1** A number of *to be* . . . phrases are expressed using **avoir** in French (for example *to be hungry* is **avoir faim**). These phrases are:

avoir . . . ans	*to be . . . years old*
avoir faim	*to be hungry*
avoir soif	*to be thirsty*

avoir chaud	to be hot
avoir froid	to be cold
avoir peur	to be frightened
avoir honte	to be ashamed
avoir raison	to be right
avoir tort	to be wrong
Quel âge a-t-il?	How old is he?

■ **44.6.2** When describing the weather, **être** is only used when the sentence starts with **le temps**:

Le temps était très mauvais.   *The weather was very bad.*

but:

Il fait froid.   *It is cold.*

■ **44.6.3** When *to be* is part of an English continuous tense (*I **am** reading, he **was** eating*), it is not translated into French. Instead, the appropriate tense (present or imperfect, see 29, 31, 40.1.3) is used:

Je ne travaille pas aujourd'hui. *I **am** not working today.*

45 Reflexive Verbs

A large number of French verbs can be used with a reflexive pronoun. Reflexive pronouns (see 26.1) refer to, or in other words, "reflect" the subject. For example, **se présenter** (*to introduce oneself*):

je me présente	**nous nous** présentons
tu te présentes	**vous vous** présentez
il/elle/on se présente	**ils/elles se** présentent

Reflexive verbs build their **passé composé** tense with **être** and the past participle (see 30):

Nous nous sommes promenés. *We went for a walk.*

45.1 Main Categories of Reflexive Verbs

■ **45.1.1** All verbs describing injuries can be used with reflexive pronouns (e.g., **se brûler**, *to burn oneself*; **se faire mal**, *to hurt oneself*, etc.).
Even when the injured part of the body is mentioned, a reflexive pronoun is used rather than a possessive adjective:

Je **me** suis coupé **le** doigt.   *I have cut **my** finger.*

■ **45.1.2** Many French verbs that describe daily activities use a reflexive pronoun when the subject is doing the action to himself or herself. Compare:

Je lave la voiture.	*I wash the car.*
Je me lave.	*I wash.*
Je baigne les enfants.	*I give the children a bath.*
Je me baigne.	*I have a bath/I swim.*
J'arrête un taxi.	*I hail a taxi.*
Je m'arrête ici.	*I stop here.*

■ **45.1.3** Some verbs used with a reflexive pronoun have the meaning of *to get*, *to become* or express a change or a development. Here are some of the most common ones:

se calmer	*to calm down*
se mettre en colère	*to get cross*
s'impatienter	*to become impatient*
se fatiguer	*to get tired*
s'améliorer	*to get better*
se développer	*to develop*
s'installer	*to settle down*
se moderniser	*to modernize*
se grouper/se former	*to form*
se transformer	*to change*

Cette ville s'est beaucoup transformée et développée en dix ans.	*This town has changed and developed a lot in ten years.*

An impersonal reflexive construction is sometimes used to express a change or a new development:

Il s'est construit une nouvelle cité.	*A new residential area has been built.*

■ **45.1.4** In many colloquial phrases telling how certain things are done or should be done, a reflexive construction is used:

Comment ça s'écrit?	*How is it written?/How do you spell it?*
Ça ne se fait pas.	*You don't do that.*
Il se lave à la machine?	*Does it go in the washing machine?*
Ce vin se boit frais.	*This wine ought to be drunk chilled.*
Ce livre se lit facilement.	*This book is easy to read.*
Ce produit se vend bien.	*This product sells well.*
Cette porte s'ouvre automatiquement.	*This door opens automatically.*

■ **45.1.5 Other Reflexive Verbs**

The following reflexive verbs are also used frequently:

se charger de	to take charge of
se dépêcher	to hurry
s'occuper de	to deal with
se souvenir de	to remember
il s'agit de	it is about, it is a question of
il se peut que	it is possible that (followed by subjunctive)
il se trouve que	it just so happens that
De quoi s'agit-il?	What is it about?
Il se peut que nous allions camper.	We may go camping.
Tu t'en souviens?	Do you remember it?

Finally, here is a selection of other common reflexive verbs with their nonreflexive equivalents: it shows how the meaning of these verbs is affected by the use of a reflexive pronoun.

Nonreflexive	Reflexive
appeler (to call)	**s'appeler** (to be called)
attendre (to wait)	**s'attendre à** (to expect)
aller (to go)	**s'en aller** (to go away)
diriger (to lead)	**se diriger vers** (to head towards)
excuser (to excuse)	**s'excuser de** (to apologize for)
demander (to ask)	**se demander** (to wonder)
mettre (to put)	**se mettre à** (to start doing something)
rappeler (to call back, to remind)	**se rappeler** (to remember)
renseigner (to inform)	**se renseigner** (to inquire)
retourner (to turn over, to go again)	**se retourner** (to turn around)
tromper (to cheat)	**se tromper** (to be mistaken)
trouver (to find)	**se trouver** (to be situated)

| Je voudrais me renseigner sur vos tarifs. | *I would like to inquire about your prices.* |
| Où se trouve l'hôtel? | *Where is the hotel?* |

45.2 Reflexive Pronouns Used for "each other"

Note that in the plural or when the subject is **on**, reflexive pronouns are also used to mean *each other* or *one another*:

Ils ne se parlent plus.	*They don't talk to one another any more.*
On se voit souvent.	*We often see each other.*
On se retrouve au café.	*We'll meet at the restaurant.*

46 Impersonal Verbs

Impersonal verbs are verbs—or verbal phrases—that can only be used in the **il** form or in the infinitive:

| Il pleut. | It is raining. |
| Il va pleuvoir. | It is going to rain. |

Here is a selection of very common impersonal verbs (for **il faut** see 44.5).

46.1 Verbs Describing the Weather

Expressions describing the weather are impersonal:

Il neige.	It is snowing.
Il fait beau/mauvais.	It's nice/bad weather.
Il fait jour/nuit.	It's daylight/dark.

46.2 How to Express "There is . . ."

■ **46.2.1 Il y a** is the most common phrase for *there is/there are* and *there was/there were*:

| Il y a beaucoup de monde. | There are a lot of people. |
| Il n'y avait pas de sucre dans le gâteau. | There was no sugar in the cake. |

The infinitive form of **il y a** is **y avoir**:

| Il doit y avoir une solution. | There must be a solution. |

■ **46.2.2 Il existe** is a more formal phrase used as an alternative to **il y a**:

| Il existe des associations qui s'occupent de cela. | There are associations dealing with that. |

■ **46.2.3 Il reste** means *there is/are left* and **il manque** means that something is lacking:

| Il reste du café? | Is there any coffee left? |
| Il manque du pain. | There isn't enough bread. |

46.3 *Il vaut mieux*

Il vaut comes from **valoir** (*to be worth*); **il vaut mieux** expresses that something is preferable or better:

Je vais les prévenir.	*I am going to warn them.*
Oui, **il vaut mieux.**	*Yes, that would be better.*

You could also say **ça vaut mieux**, or **il/ça vaudrait mieux**. It can be followed by an infinitive or **que** + subjunctive:

Il vaut mieux partir tôt.	*It's better to leave early.*
Il vaut mieux qu'elle ne vienne pas.	*It's better if she doesn't come.*

46.4 *Il paraît que, il semble que, on dirait que*

■ **46.4.1 Il paraît que** means *I have heard that* or *it appears that*:

Il paraît qu'ils ont beaucoup de succès.	*I have heard they are very successful.*

■ **46.4.2 Il semble que** is the traditional way of saying *it seems that, it looks like*. In modern colloquial French, however, the phrase **on dirait que** is used instead:

On dirait qu'il va pleuvoir.　*It looks as if it is going to rain.*

However, **il me semble que** is still used frequently:

Il me semble qu'il exagère. *It seems to me that he is going too far.*

46.5 *Il suffit*

This is a very common phrase which means *you need only to/just have to*:

Il suffit de remplir cette fiche. *You need only to complete this form.*

46.6 Reflexive Impersonal Forms

■ **46.6.1 Il s'agit de** is used to express:

- what something is about or what it is a question of:
  De quoi s'agit-il?   *What is it about?*
  Il s'agit de ma candidature. *It's about my application.*

- what is important:
  Il s'agit maintenant de   *It is important now to make*
  faire des progrès.   *some progress.*

- who someone is:
  Il s'agit de quelqu'un de   *We are talking about a very*
  très compétent.   *competent person.*

■ **46.6.2** *Il se trouve que*
Il se trouve que means it just so happens that:
  Il se trouve que j'en ai   *It just so happens that I have*
  un ici.   *one here.*

■ **46.6.3** *Il se peut que* is often used instead of **il est possible que**. Both phrases are followed by the subjunctive:
  Il se peut que nous   *We may go to Italy.*
  allions en Italie.

■ **46.6.4** Other Reflexive Constructions
Reflexive verbs that convey a change are often used in an impersonal way:
  Il s'est formé des   *Renters' associations have*
  associations de quartier.   *been set up.*

46.7 A Question of Style

A construction with **il** is also sometimes used with certain verbs of movement to emphasize the movement:
  Il me vient une idée.   *I have an idea coming.*
  Il passe beaucoup de   *A lot of cars drive down this*
  voitures dans cette rue.   *street.*

47 Verbs Used with Objects

Note the use of the abbreviations **qc** for **quelque chose** (sth, *something*) and **qn** for **quelqu'un** (sb, *someone, somebody*).

47.1 Verbs and Direct Objects

In the sentence **J'achète un journal**, **J'** is the subject, **achète** is the verb, and **un journal** is the direct object. If in response to a statement you can ask **Qu'est-ce que?** or **Qui est-ce qui?**, the verb in that statement takes a direct object. For example:

Il regarde sa montre. *He is looking at his watch.*

Qu'est-ce qu'il regarde? Sa montre: sa montre is the direct object.

J'ai rencontré M. Bernard hier matin. *I met Mr. Bernard yesterday morning.*

Qui est-ce que j'ai rencontré? M. Bernard: M. Bernard is the direct object.

A few verbs take a direct object in French, but not in English:

attendre	*to wait for*
chercher	*to look for*
demander	*to ask for*
écouter	*to listen to*
espérer	*to hope for*
essayer	*to try on*
habiter	*to live in*
mettre	*to put on*
payer	*to pay for*
regarder	*to look at*
reprocher	*to blame for*

J'attends le bus. *I am waiting for the bus.*

47.2 Verbs That Take *à* + an Object

When the verb and its object are linked by a preposition—
such as **à**—the object is an indirect object:

J'écris **à** ma copine.	*I am writing to my girlfriend.*

■ **47.2.1** In most cases, **à** is translated by *to* in English. For
example:

dire qc à qn	*to say sth to sb, to tell sb*
donner qc à qn	*to give sth to sb*
écrire qc à qn	*to write sth to sb*
envoyer qc à qn	*to send sth to sb*
montrer qc à qn	*to show sth to sb*
parler à qn	*to speak to sb*
permettre qc à qn	*to allow sb sth*
proposer qc à qn	*to propose sth to sb*
répondre à qn	*to reply to sb*

Je vais envoyer une carte	*I am going to send a card*
à mes parents.	*to my parents.*

Note that **à** cannot be dropped like *to* often is in English:
I am going to send my parents a card.

■ **47.2.2** A small number of French verbs take an indirect
object where the English takes a direct object. The most
common ones are:

demander qc à qn	*to ask sb for sth*
téléphoner à	*to phone sb*
jouer à/de	*to play sth*

(**Jouer** uses **à** for games: **ils jouent aux échecs**, *they are
playing chess*; **de** for instruments: **elle joue de la guitare**,
she plays the guitar.)

You may also need to know:

convenir à	*to suit sb*

s'attendre à	*to expect sth*
obéir à	*to obey sb*
pardonner à	*to forgive sb*
plaire à	*to please sb*
renoncer à	*to give up sth*
répondre à	*to answer sth/sb*
ressembler à	*to look like sb*

Cette date ne leur convient pas.	*This date does not suit them.*
Cela lui a beaucoup plu.	*He/she liked it a lot.*

Note also that **manquer à qn** (*to miss*) has a totally different construction from the English:

Paris lui manque beaucoup. *He/she misses Paris a lot.*

■ **47.2.3** A few verbs take **à** before an object where the English might lead you to expect a different preposition:

croire à	*to believe in*
s'intéresser à	*to be interested in*
penser/songer à	*to think of/about*
réfléchir à	*to think about*
servir à	*to be used for*

Verbs expressing *obtaining something from somebody* belong to this category:

acheter qc à qn	*to buy sth from sb*
cacher qc à qn	*to hide sth from sb*
emprunter qc à qn	*to borrow sth from sb*

47.3 Verbs That Take *de* + an Object

Some verbs take **de** before an object. The most common ones are:

avoir besoin de	*to need*
avoir envie de	*to feel like*
avoir peur de	*to be frightened of*

dépendre de	to *depend on*
parler de	to *speak of/about*
remercier qn de	to *thank sb for*
s'occuper de	to *deal with, to look after*
se servir de	to *use*
se souvenir de	to *remember*
se tromper de	to *be mistaken over*

Je me suis trompé de numéro.	*I dialed the wrong number.*
Nous vous remercions de votre lettre du 2 février.	*Thank you for your letter of February 2.*

You may also need to know:

s'apercevoir de	to *notice*
s'approcher de	to *come near*
changer de	to *change*
discuter de	to *discuss*
douter de	to *doubt*
féliciter de	to *congratulate for*
jouir de	to *enjoy*
manquer de	to *lack*
se méfier de	to *mistrust*
rire de	to *laugh at*
traiter de	to *be about/to deal with*
vivre de	to *live on*

48 Verbs Used with Infinitives

Often when a verb follows another verb, the second verb is used in the infinitive. This is not always the case in English: **Je ne pouvais pas m'arrêter de rire**. (*I couldn't stop laughing.*)

There are four types of constructions when the infinitive follows a verb:

- verb + infinitive
- verb + **à** + infinitive
- verb + **de** + infinitive
- verb + **par** + infinitive

The construction that is used is determined by the first verb. It is therefore important to learn each verb with its following preposition, if it has one.

48.1 Verbs That Take an Infinitive Without a Preposition

Verbs followed by an infinitive without a preposition are:

- **devoir** (*to have to*), **pouvoir** (*to be able to*), **vouloir** (*to want to*), **savoir** (*to know*), **il faut** (*to have to*):
  Nous pouvons partir.   *We can go.*

- verbs of likes and dislikes:
  J'aime marcher.   *I like walking.*

- verbs of wish and willing:
  J'espère les voir demain.   *I hope to see them tomorrow.*

- Verbs of perception (**entendre**, *to hear*; **voir**, *to see*, etc.)
  Je l'entends venir.   *I can hear him coming.*

- Some verbs of movement (**aller**, *to go*; **descendre**, *to descend*; **monter**, *to climb*; **partir**, *to leave*; **sortir**, *to go out*; and **venir**, *to come*):

| Je vais partir. | *I am going to leave.* |
| Venez nous voir! | *Come and see us!* |

- **faire** and **laisser**: **faire** means either *to make someone do something* or *to have something done*; **laisser** means *to let someone do something*:

Faites-le entrer!	*Show him in!*
Fais-le travailler!	*Make him work!*
Je l'ai fait réparer.	*I had it repaired.*
Je l'ai laissé partir.	*I let him go.*

- Also note the following common expressions:

aller chercher	*to go and get*
venir chercher	*to come and get/to pick up*
entendre dire que	*to hear that*
entendre parler de	*to hear of/about*
laisser tomber	*to drop*
vouloir dire	*to mean*

| Je vais aller les chercher | *I am going to pick them up at* |
| à la gare. | *the station.* |

48.2 Verbs That Take *à* + an Infinitive

The most common verbs that can be followed by **à** and an infinitive are:

aider à	*to help to*
s'amuser à	*to have fun doing sth*
apprendre à	*to learn to*
apprendre à qn à	*to teach sb to*
arriver à	*to manage to*
s'attendre à	*to expect to*
autoriser à	*to allow to*
avoir à	*to have to*
chercher à	*to try to*
commencer à	*to begin to*

consentir à	to consent to
consister à	to consist of
continuer à	to continue to
encourager à	to encourage to
forcer à	to force to
hésiter à	to hesitate to
se mettre à	to start to
obliger à	to force to
penser à	to think of
persister à	to persist in
pousser à	to urge to
se préparer à	to get ready to
renoncer à	to renounce sth
réussir à	to succeed in
rester à	to remain to
servir à	to be used for
tarder à	to be late for
tenir à	to be eager to

Je lui ai appris à conduire.	I taught him/her how to drive.
Je n'arrive pas à fermer ma valise.	I can't manage to close my suitcase.
Je tiens à vous remercier de votre hospitalité.	I wish to thank you for your hospitality.

48.3 Verbs That Take *de* + an Infinitive

Below is a list of the most common verbs that can be followed by **de** + infinitive.

accepter de	to accept
accuser de	to accuse of
arrêter de	to stop doing sth
avoir besoin de	to need to

avoir envie de	to feel like doing sth
avoir peur de	to be frightened of
cesser de	to stop doing sth
se charger de	to take charge of
conseiller de	to advise to
convenir de	to suit to
craindre de	to fear doing sth
décider de	to decide to
défendre de	to forbid to
demander de	to ask to
se dépêcher de	to hurry to
dire de	to say/to tell to
empêcher de	to hinder from
essayer de	to try to
s'étonner de	to be surprised to
éviter de	to avoid doing sth
s'excuser de	to apologize for
finir de	to finish doing sth
interdire de	to forbid to
menacer de	to threaten to
mériter de	to deserve to
s'occuper de	to deal with
offrir de	to offer/to give to
ordonner de	to order to
oublier de	to forget to
permettre de	to allow to
persuader de	to convince to
prier de	to beg to
promettre de	to promise to
proposer de	to propose/suggest/offer that
rappeler de	to remind to
se rappeler de	to remember to
recommander de	to recommend that
refuser de	to refuse to

regretter de	to regret that
remercier de	to thank for
se souvenir de	to remember doing sth
suggérer de	to suggest that

| Je vous prie de m'excuser. | Would you please excuse me? |
| J'ai envie d'aller me baigner. | I feel like going for a swim. |

For the use of **venir de**, see 29.4.4.

48.4 Verbs That Take *par* + an Infinitive

Commencer (*to begin*) and **finir** (*to finish*) are followed by **par** when they mean *to start/finish* **with**:

| On va commencer par tout ranger. | We'll start with tidying up everything. |
| Je finis par m'ennuyer. | I get bored in the end. |

49 Linking Words

There are two categories of linking words or conjunctions: coordinating conjunctions (words like **et**, *and*; **mais**, *but*, etc.) and subordinating conjunctions (words like **parce que**, *because*; **si**, *if*, etc.).

49.1 Coordinating Conjunctions

Coordinating conjunctions are words that link words or groups of words of equal status (e.g., nouns to nouns, main clauses to main clauses, subordinate clauses to subordinate clauses). The most common ones are:

mais	*but*
ou	*or*
et	*and*
donc	*therefore/so*
or	*however*
ni… ni…	*neither*
car	*because*
cependant	*however*
pourtant	*however*
toutefois	*however*
soit… soit…	*either . . . or . . .*
au contraire	*on the contrary*
néanmoins	*nevertheless*
en effet	*indeed*
d'ailleurs	*besides*
c'est-à-dire	*that is to say*
à savoir	*that is, i.e.*
ainsi	*thus*
aussi	*so*
c'est pourquoi	*that's why*

Nous sommes rentrés ravis mais fatigués.	*We came back feeling happy but tired.*

J'ai un examen demain, je vais donc passer la soirée à étudier.	*I have an exam tomorrow so I will spend this evening studying.*
Je ne pourrai pas les recevoir en personne **car** je serai absent ce jour-là.	*I won't be able to welcome them myself because I won't be in on that day.*

In clauses beginning with **aussi**, the verb comes before the subject (see 50.1.3):

Aussi faut-il être prudent!	*So we have to be careful!*

49.2 Subordinating Conjunctions

■ **49.2.1** These link a subordinate clause to a main clause. A subordinate clause cannot exist without a main clause. Its function is to expand upon the meaning of the main clause:

Je l'aime **parce qu'il a un** beau sourire.	*I love him because he has a beautiful smile.*

The most common subordinating conjunctions are:

que	*that*	malgré que*	*although*
quand	*when*	sans que*	*unless*
lorsque	*when*	tandis que	*while*
avant que*	*before*	à moins que*	*unless*
aussitôt que	*as soon as*	comme	*as/since*
dès que	*as soon as*	parce que	*because*
depuis que	*since*	puisque	*since*
après que	*after*	afin que*	*so that*
jusqu'à ce que*	*until*	pour que*	*so that*
pendant que	*while*	de peur que*	*for fear that*
en attendant que*	*while*	de sorte que**	*so that*
à mesure que	*while*	de façon que**	*so that*
bien que*	*although*	de manière que**	*so that*
quoique*	*although*	tellement que	*so much that*
alors que	*while*	si	*if/whether*

étant donné que	*given the fact that*
au cas où	*in case that*
à condition que*	*on condition that*
pourvu que*	*provided that*
de même que	*in the same way as*

Je viendrai demain **pour que** tu ne sois pas seule.	*I'll come tomorrow so that you won't be alone.*
Tout lui réussit **tandis que** moi, je n'ai jamais de veine.	*He succeeds in everything while I am never lucky.*

* The conjunctions with one asterisk are always followed by the subjunctive (see 43).

** The conjunctions with two asterisks are followed by the subjunctive when they express purpose (as opposed to consequence):

Il nous a longuement parlé de sorte que nous **comprenions** bien la situation.	*He talked to us at length to help us to understand the situation.*

but:

Il a parlé très clairement de sorte que nous n'**avons** pas **eu** de mal à le comprendre.	*He talked very clearly so that it was easy to understand him.*

■ **49.2.2** When a conjunction introduces more than one verb, **que** is used to introduce the second (and subsequent) clause(s):

Comme tu t'intéresses à la philatélie **et que** tu n'es pas pressé, je vais te montrer ce que j'ai reçu hier.	*Since you are interested in stamps and you are not in a hurry, I will show you what I received yesterday.*

50 Word Order

Word order is by and large similar in French and in English—the most common pattern is subject + verb + object. This section summarizes the cases where French and English word order differ.

50.1 Inversion

■ **50.1.1** The subject and verb can be inverted in direct questions, but do not have to be (see 20.1):

Etes-vous allés au Pont du Gard?   *Did you go to the Pont du Gard?*

■ **50.1.2** The verb and noun are inverted in indirect questions when the subject is a noun and the verb would otherwise be at the end of the sentence (see 20.3):

J'ai demandé au monsieur où se trouve la piscine.   *I asked the man where the swimming pool is.*

■ **50.1.3** When a clause starts with **peut-être** (*perhaps*), **à peine** (*hardly*), or **aussi** (*so*), the verb and the subject pronoun are inverted:

Peut-être a-t-il eu des ennuis.   *Perhaps he got into trouble.*

A peine avait-elle commencé à lire la lettre qu'elle devint toute pâle.   *She had hardly started reading the letter when she went very pale.*

Aussi mon père est-il content de nous.   *So my father is pleased with us.*

In everyday French, however, the inversion is often avoided by placing **peut-être** and **à peine** after the verb or by using **peut-être que**:

Peut-être qu'il a eu des ennuis./Il a peut-être eu des ennuis.   *Perhaps he got into trouble.*

| Elle avait à peine commencé à lire la lettre qu'elle devint toute pâle. | *She had hardly started reading the letter when she went very pale.* |

■ **50.1.4** After direct speech, the subject and the verb of saying are inverted:

| "Quelle belle journée!" dit-il. | *"What a beautiful day!" he said.* |

50.2 No Change of Word Order

■ **50.2.1** There is no change of word order in exclamations:

| Qu'il fait chaud! | *Isn't it hot!* |

■ **50.2.2** After **dont**, the normal word order of subject + verb + object is used, which is not always the case in English (see 27.5):

| C'est Pierre dont tu as déjà rencontré les parents. | *This is Pierre, whose parents you have already met.* |

50.3 Other Differences Between French and English Word Order

■ **50.3.1** Adjectives usually come after the noun (see 12 for exceptions):

| Vous avez un journal anglais? | *Do you have an English newspaper?* |

■ **50.3.2** Adverbs usually come after the verb (see 15):

| Il frappe toujours avant d'entrer. | *He always knocks before coming in.* |

■ **50.3.3** Object pronouns come before the verb, except in a positive command (see 23.3):

| Je le lui ai donné. | *I have given it to him/her.* |

■ **50.3.4** Most negatives go around the verb:
Je **n'**ai **pas** de sucre.   *I don't have any sugar.*

Ne comes before any object pronoun:
Elle ne s'achète jamais   *She never buys herself any*
de fleurs.   *flowers.*

See 21.2 for more details on word order in negative
expressions.

■ **50.3.5** A noun phrase is a combination of two nouns.
In French, they are linked with **de**, **à**, or **en** and come in
the opposite order to English noun phrases:
la voiture de mon frère   *my brother's car*
un magasin de chaussures   *a shoe store*
un verre en plastique   *a plastic glass*
un verre à vin   *a wine glass*

51 Conjugation of Regular Verbs

51.1 Endings

Within a tense nearly all verbs—whether regular or irregular—have the same endings. For most irregular verbs, the irregularity occurs within the stem, not at the ending. The verb endings are as follows:

	Present	Imperfect and Conditional	Future	Present subjunctive
je	-e *or* -s	-ais	-ai	-e
tu	-es -s	-ais	-as	-es
il/elle/on	-e -t	-ait	-a	-e
nous	-ons	-ions	-ons	-ions
vous	-ez	-iez	-ez	-iez
ils/elles	-ent	-aient	-ont	-ent

The **passé simple** has these endings:

	Verbs in -**er**	Verbs in -**ir**, and some other verbs	Other common endings
je	-ai	-is	-us
tu	-as	-is	-us
il/elle/on	-a	-it	-ut
nous	-âmes	-îmes	-ûmes
vous	-âtes	-îtes	-ûtes
ils/elles	-èrent	-irent	-urent

51.2 Stems

The above endings are added to the stem of the verb, which can vary according to the tense or mood. You'll find more detailed explanations in 29–43, but here is a general guideline:

■ 51.2.1 Present
The stem of verbs ending in **-er** is given by the infinitive form without **-er**: the stem of **donner** is **donn**-.

The stems of some verbs ending in **-ir** follow the same pattern as **finir** (see 29.2): they are found by removing the **-ir**: the stem of **finir** is **fin**—in the singular; the plural stem is **finiss**-.

The majority of the other verbs show irregularities within their stems and need to be learned individually.

■ 51.2.2 Imperfect
The stem is given by the present tense **nous** form without the **-ons** ending (see 31): So the imperfect of **prendre** is **je prenais** (from nous **pren**ons).

■ 51.2.3 Future and Conditional Present
The stem is the same as in the infinitive, though the **-e** in **-re** verbs is dropped (see 35 and 37).

■ 51.2.4 Subjunctive Present
The **nous** and **vous** forms are the same as in the imperfect. The stem for the other forms is given by the present tense **ils** form.

■ 51.2.5 *Passé Simple*
Verbs ending in **-er** and **-ir** use their infinitive without the **-er** or **-ir** ending.
Other verbs use different types of stems, and need therefore to be learned individually.

Irregular Verbs

Some verbs are irregular. This means that their stems (or occasionally endings) do not follow the regular pattern in all parts of the verb. Even irregular verbs follow patterns, however, so listed below is the full conjugation of the present tense indicative, and the **je** forms of the other tenses and moods. You can derive the other forms from this **je** form by adding the regular endings listed in 51. For example, if you know the future **je** form of **aller** is **j'irai**, you can work out the **nous** form (**nous irons**) by adding the standard -**ons** ending to the stem **ir-**.

A few verbs have extra irregularities: in the present subjunctive **avoir** changes its stem in the **nous** and **vous** forms. To show this, its subjunctive forms are listed in full.

The imperative is given only if it is irregular.

We have listed **aller** in full to illustrate how even irregular verbs use regular endings.

52.1 Aller (*to go*)

PRESENT	IMPERFECT	PRESENT CONDITIONAL
je vais	j'allais	j'irais
tu vas	tu allais	tu irais
il va	il allait	il irait
nous allons	nous allions	nous irions
vous allez	vous alliez	vous iriez
ils vont	ils allaient	ils iraient

PASSÉ COMPOSÉ	FUTURE	PAST CONDITIONAL
je suis allé	j'irai	je serais allé
tu es allé	tu iras	tu serais allé
il est allé	il ira	il serait allé
nous sommes allés	nous irons	nous serions allés
vous êtes allés	vous irez	vous seriez allés
ils sont allés	ils iront	ils seraient allés

PRESENT SUBJUNCTIVE	PASSÉ SIMPLE	IMPERATIVE
j'aille	j'allai	va (**vas** before **y**)
tu ailles	tu allas	allons
il aille	il alla	allez
nous allions	nous allâmes	
vous alliez	vous allâtes	
ils aillent	ils allèrent	

52.2 S'asseoir (*to sit down*)

PRESENT
je m'assois/assieds*
tu t'assois/assieds*
il s'assoit/assied*
nous nous asseyons
vous vous asseyez
ils s'assoient/
   asseyent*

*Both forms are
used.

PASSÉ COMPOSÉ
je me suis assis

IMPERFECT
je m'asseyais

FUTURE
je m'assiérai

PRESENT CONDITIONAL
je m'assiérais

PAST CONDITIONAL
je me serais assis

PRESENT SUBJUNCTIVE
je m'asseye

PASSÉ SIMPLE
je m'assis

52.3 Avoir (*to have*)

PRESENT
j'ai
tu as
il a
nous avons
vous avez
ils ont

PASSÉ COMPOSÉ
j'ai eu

IMPERFECT
j'avais

FUTURE
j'aurai

PRESENT CONDITIONAL
j'aurais

PAST CONDTIONAL
j'aurais eu

PRESENT SUBJUNCTIVE
j'aie
tu aies
il ait

nous ayons
vous ayez
ils aient

PASSÉ SIMPLE
j'eus

IMPERATIVE
aie
ayons
ayez

52.4 Battre* (*to fight*)

PRESENT	IMPERFECT	PRESENT SUBJUNCTIVE
je bats	je battais	je batte
tu bats		
il bat	FUTURE	PASSÉ SIMPLE
nous battons	je battrai	je battis
vous battez	PRESENT CONDITIONAL	*Also **combattre**
ils battent	je battrais	(*to fight*)
PASSÉ COMPOSÉ	PAST CONDITIONAL	
j'ai battu	j'aurais battu	

52.5 Boire (*to drink*)

PRESENT	IMPERFECT	PRESENT SUBJUNCTIVE
je bois	je buvais	je boive
tu bois		nous buvions
il boit	FUTURE	vous buviez
nous buvons	je boirai	
vous buvez	PRESENT CONDITIONAL	PASSÉ SIMPLE
ils boivent	je boirais	je bus
PASSÉ COMPOSÉ	PAST CONDITIONAL	
j'ai bu	j'aurais bu	

52.6 Conduire (*to drive*)

PRESENT	IMPERFECT	PRESENT SUBJUNCTIVE
je conduis	je conduisais	je conduise
tu conduis		
il conduit	FUTURE	PASSÉ SIMPLE
nous conduisons	je conduirai	je conduisis
vous conduisez	PRESENT CONDITIONAL	
ils conduisent	je conduirais	
PASSÉ COMPOSÉ	PAST CONDITIONAL	
j'ai conduit	j'aurais conduit	

52.7 Connaître (*to know*)

PRESENT	IMPERFECT	PRESENT SUBJUNCTIVE
je connais	je connaissais	je connaisse
tu connais		
il connaît	FUTURE	PASSÉ SIMPLE
nous connaissons	je connaîtrai	je connus
vous connaissez	PRESENT CONDITIONAL	
ils connaissent	je connaîtrais	

PASSÉ COMPOSÉ   PAST CONDITIONAL
j'ai connu   j'aurais connu

52.8 Coudre (*to sew*)

PRESENT	IMPERFECT	PRESENT SUBJUNCTIVE
je couds	je cousais	je couse
tu couds		
il coud	FUTURE	PASSÉ SIMPLE
nous cousons	je coudrai	je cousis
vous cousez	PRESENT CONDITIONAL	
ils cousent	je coudrais	

PASSÉ COMPOSÉ   PAST CONDITIONAL
j'ai cousu   j'aurais cousu

52.9 Courir (*to run*)

PRESENT	IMPERFECT	PRESENT SUBJUNCTIVE
je cours	je courais	je coure
tu cours		
il court	FUTURE	PASSÉ SIMPLE
nous courons	je courrai	je courus
vous courez	PRESENT CONDITIONAL	
ils courent	je courrais	

PASSÉ COMPOSÉ   PAST CONDITIONAL
j'ai couru   j'aurais couru

52.10 Craindre* (*to fear*)

PRESENT	IMPERFECT	PRESENT SUBJUNCTIVE
je crains	je craignais	je craigne
tu crains		
il craint	FUTURE	PASSÉ SIMPLE
nous craignons	je craindrai	je craignis
vous craignez	PRESENT CONDITIONAL	*Also other verbs
ils craignent	je craindrais	ending in **-aindre**
PASSÉ COMPOSÉ	PAST CONDITIONAL	
j'ai craint	j'aurais craint	

52.11 Croire (*to believe*)

PRESENT	IMPERFECT	PRESENT SUBJUNCTIVE
je crois	je croyais	je croie
tu crois		nous croyions
il croit	FUTURE	vous croyiez
nous croyons	je croirai	
vous croyez	PRESENT CONDITIONAL	PASSÉ SIMPLE
ils croient	je croirais	je crus
PASSÉ COMPOSÉ	PAST CONDITIONAL	
j'ai cru	j'aurais cru	

52.12 Cueillir* (*to pick*)

PRESENT	IMPERFECT	PRESENT SUBJUNCTIVE
je cueille	je cueillais	je cueille
tu cueilles		
il cueille	FUTURE	PASSÉ SIMPLE
nous cueillons	je cueillerai	je cueillis
vous cueillez	PRESENT CONDITIONAL	* Also **accueillir**
ils cueillent	je cueillerais	(*to greet*) and
		recueillir (*to*
PASSÉ COMPOSÉ	PAST CONDITIONAL	*collect*)
j'ai cueilli	j'aurais cueilli	

52.13 Cuire* (*to cook*)

PRESENT	IMPERFECT	PRESENT SUBJUNCTIVE
je cuis	je cuisais	je cuise
tu cuis		
il cuit	FUTURE	PASSÉ SIMPLE
nous cuisons	je cuirai	je cuisis
vous cuisez		
ils cuisent	PRESENT CONDITIONAL	*Also other verbs
	je cuirais	ending in **-uire**
PASSÉ COMPOSÉ	PAST CONDITIONAL	
j'ai cuit	j'aurais cuit	

52.14 Devoir (*to have to/to owe*)

PRESENT	IMPERFECT	PRESENT SUBJUNCTIVE
je dois	je devais	je doive
tu dois		nous devions
il doit	FUTURE	vous deviez
nous devons	je devrai	
vous devez	PAST CONDITIONAL	PASSÉ SIMPLE
ils doivent	je devrais	je dus
PASSÉ COMPOSÉ	PAST CONDITIONAL	PAST PARTICIPLE
j'ai dû	j'aurais dû	dû, due,
		dus, dues

52.15 Dire (*to say*)

PRESENT	IMPERFECT	PRESENT SUBJUNCTIVE
je dis	je disais	je dise
tu dis		
il dit	FUTURE	PASSÉ SIMPLE
nous disons	je dirai	je dis
vous dites		
ils disent	PRESENT CONDITIONAL	
	je dirais	
PASSÉ COMPOSÉ	PAST CONDITIONAL	
j'ai dit	j'aurais dit	

52.16 Dormir (*to sleep*)

PRESENT
je dors
tu dors
il dort
nous dormons
vous dormez
ils dorment

PASSÉ COMPOSÉ
j'ai dormi

IMPERFECT
je dormais

FUTURE
je dormirai

PRESENT CONDITIONAL
je dormirais

PAST CONDITIONAL
j'aurais dormi

PRESENT SUBJUNCTIVE
je dorme

PASSÉ SIMPLE
je dormis

52.17 Écrire (*to write*)

PRESENT
j'écris
tu écris
il écrit
nous écrivons
vous écrivez
ils écrivent

PASSÉ COMPOSÉ
j'ai écrit

IMPERFECT
j'écrivais

FUTURE
j'écrirai

PRESENT CONDITIONAL
j'écrirais

PAST CONDITIONAL
j'aurais écrit

PRESENT SUBJUNCTIVE
j'écrive

PASSÉ SIMPLE
j'écrivis

52.18 Envoyer (*to send*)

PRESENT
j'envoie
tu envoies
il envoie
nous envoyons
vous envoyez
ils envoient

PASSÉ COMPOSÉ
j'ai envoyé

IMPERFECT
j'envoyais

FUTURE
j'enverrai

PRESENT CONDITIONAL
j'enverrais

PAST CONDITIONAL
j'aurais envoyé

PRESENT SUBJUNCTIVE
j'envoie

PASSÉ SIMPLE
j'envoyai

52.19 Être (*to be*)

PRESENT	IMPERFECT	PRESENT SUBJUNCTIVE
je suis	j'étais	je sois
tu es		nous soyons
il est	FUTURE	vous soyez
nous sommes	je serai	ils soient
vous êtes		
ils sont	PRESENT CONDITIONAL	PASSÉ SIMPLE
	je serais	je fus
PASSÉ COMPOSÉ	PAST CONDITIONAL	IMPERATIVE
j'ai été	j'aurais été	sois
		soyons
		soyez

52.20 Faire (*to do/to make*)

PRESENT	IMPERFECT	PRESENT SUBJUNCTIVE
je fais	je faisais	je fasse
tu fais		
il fait	FUTURE	PASSÉ SIMPLE
nous faisons	je ferai	je fis
vous faites		
ils font	PRESENT CONDITIONAL	
	je ferais	
PASSÉ COMPOSÉ	PAST CONDITIONAL	
j'ai fait	j'aurais fait	

52.21 Falloir (*to be necessary*)

PRESENT	FUTURE	PRESENT SUBJUNCTIVE
il faut	il faudra	il faille
PASSÉ COMPOSÉ	PRESENT CONDITIONAL	PASSÉ SIMPLE
il a fallu	il faudrait	il fallut
IMPERFECT	PAST CONDITIONAL	
il fallait	il aurait fallu	

52.22 Haïr (to hate)

PRESENT
je hais
tu hais
il hait
nous haïssons
vous haïssez
ils haïssent

PASSÉ COMPOSÉ
j'ai haï

IMPERFECT
je haïssais

FUTURE
je haïrai

PRESENT CONDITIONAL
je haïrais

PAST CONDITIONAL
j'aurais haï

PRESENT SUBJUNCTIVE
je haïsse

PASSÉ SIMPLE
je haïs

52.23 Lire (to read)

PRESENT
je lis
tu lis
il lit
nous lisons
vous lisez
ils lisent

PASSÉ COMPOSÉ
j'ai lu

IMPERFECT
je lisais

FUTURE
je lirai

PRESENT CONDITIONAL
je lirais

PAST CONDITIONAL
j'aurais lu

PRESENT SUBJUNCTIVE
je lise

PASSÉ SIMPLE
je lus

52.24 Mettre (to put)

PRESENT
je mets
tu mets
il met
nous mettons
vous mettez
ils mettent

PASSÉ COMPOSÉ
j'ai mis

IMPERFECT
je mettais

FUTURE
je mettrai

PRESENT CONDITIONAL
je mettrais

PAST CONDITIONAL
j'aurais mis

PRESENT SUBJUNCTIVE
je mette

PASSÉ SIMPLE
je mis

52.25 Mourir (*to die*)

PRESENT	IMPERFECT	PRESENT SUBJUNCTIVE
je meurs	je mourais	je meure
tu meurs		nous mourions
il meurt	FUTURE	vous mouriez
nous mourons	je mourrai	
vous mourez		PASSÉ SIMPLE
ils meurent	PRESENT CONDITIONAL	je mourus
	je mourrais	
PASSÉ COMPOSÉ	PAST CONDITIONAL	
je suis mort	je serais mort	

52.26 Naître (*to be born*)

PRESENT	IMPERFECT	PRESENT SUBJUNCTIVE
je nais	je naissais	je naisse
tu nais		
il naît	FUTURE	PASSÉ SIMPLE
nous naissons	je naîtrai	je naquis
vous naissez		
ils naissent	PRESENT CONDITIONAL	
	je naîtrais	
PASSÉ COMPOSÉ	PAST CONDITIONAL	
je suis né	je serais né	

52.27 Ouvrir* (*to open*)

PRESENT	IMPERFECT	PRESENT SUBJUNCTIVE
j'ouvre	j'ouvrais	j'ouvre
tu ouvres		
il ouvre	FUTURE	PASSÉ SIMPLE
nous ouvrons	j'ouvrirai	j'ouvris
vous ouvrez		
ils ouvrent	PRESENT CONDITIONAL	*Also **offrir** (*to*
	j'ouvrirais	*offer*) and
PASSÉ COMPOSÉ	PAST CONDITIONAL	**découvrir** (*to*
j'ai ouvert	j'aurais ouvert	*discover*)

52.28 Paraître* (*to appear*)

PRESENT
je parais
tu parais
il paraît
nous paraissons
vous paraissez
ils paraissent

PASSÉ COMPOSÉ
j'ai paru

IMPERFECT
je paraissais

FUTURE
je paraîtrai

PRESENT CONDITIONAL
je paraîtrais

PAST CONDITIONAL
j'aurais paru

PRESENT SUBJUNCTIVE
je paraisse

PASSÉ SIMPLE
je parus

*Also **apparaître**
(*to appear*)

52.29 Partir (*to leave*)

PRESENT
je pars
tu pars
il part
nous partons
vous partez
ils partent

PASSÉ COMPOSÉ
je suis parti

IMPERFECT
je partais

FUTURE
je partirai

PRESENT CONDITIONAL
je partirais

PAST CONDITIONAL
je serais parti

PRESENT SUBJUNCTIVE
je parte

PASSÉ SIMPLE
je partis

52.30 Peindre* (*to paint*)

PRESENT
je peins
tu peins
il peint
nous peignons
vous peignez
ils peignent

PASSÉ COMPOSÉ
j'ai peint

IMPERFECT
je peignais

FUTURE
je peindrai

PRESENT CONDITIONAL
je peindrais

PAST CONDITIONAL
j'aurais peint

PRESENT SUBJUNCTIVE
je peigne

PASSÉ SIMPLE
je peignis

*Also other verbs
ending in
-eindre

52.31 Plaire (*to be likeable/to please*)

PRESENT	IMPERFECT	PRESENT SUBJUNCTIVE
je plais	je plaisais	je plaise
tu plais		
il plaît	FUTURE	PASSÉ SIMPLE
nous plaisons	je plairai	je plus
vous plaisez		
ils plaisent	PRESENT CONDITIONAL	
	je plairais	
PASSÉ COMPOSÉ	PAST CONDITIONAL	
j'ai plu	j'aurais plu	

52.32 Pleuvoir (*to rain*)

PRESENT	FUTURE	PRESENT SUBJUNCTIVE
il pleut	il pleuvra	il pleuve
PASSÉ COMPOSÉ	PRESENT CONDITIONAL	PASSÉ SIMPLE
il a plu	il pleuvrait	il plut
IMPERFECT	PAST CONDITIONAL	
il pleuvait	il aurait plu	

52.33 Pouvoir (*to be able to*)

PRESENT	IMPERFECT	PRESENT SUBJUNCTIVE
je peux	je pouvais	je puisse
tu peux		
il peut	FUTURE	PASSÉ SIMPLE
nous pouvons	je pourrai	je pus
vous pouvez		
ils peuvent	PRESENT CONDITIONAL	
	je pourrais	
PASSÉ COMPOSÉ	PAST CONDITIONAL	
j'ai pu	j'aurais pu	

52.34 Prendre* (*to take*)

PRESENT
je prends
tu prends
il prend
nous prenons
vous prenez
ils prennent

PASSÉ COMPOSÉ
j'ai pris

IMPERFECT
je prenais

FUTURE
je prendrai

PRESENT CONDITIONAL
je prendrais

PAST CONDITIONAL
j'aurais pris

PRESENT SUBJUNCTIVE
je prenne

PASSÉ SIMPLE
je pris

*Also **apprendre** (*to learn/teach*); **comprendre** (*to understand*); and **méprendre** (*to be mistaken*)

52.35 Recevoir* (*to receive*)

PRESENT
je reçois
tu reçois
il reçoit
nous recevons
vous recevez
ils reçoivent

PASSÉ COMPOSÉ
j'ai reçu

IMPERFECT
je recevais

FUTURE
je recevrai

PRESENT CONDITIONAL
je recevrais

PAST CONDITIONAL
j'aurais reçu

PRESENT SUBJUNCTIVE
je reçoive
nous recevions
vous receviez

PASSÉ SIMPLE
je reçus

*Also **apercevoir** (*to glimpse*)

52.36 Résoudre (*to solve*)

PRESENT
je résous
tu résous
il résout
nous résolvons
vous résolvez
ils résolvent

PASSÉ COMPOSÉ
j'ai résolu

IMPERFECT
je résolvais

FUTURE
je résoudrai

PRESENT CONDITIONAL
je résoudrais

PAST CONDITIONAL
j'aurais résolu

PRESENT SUBJUNCTIVE
je résolve

PASSÉ SIMPLE
je résolus

52.37 Rire (*to laugh*)

PRESENT	IMPERFECT	PRESENT SUBJUNCTIVE
je ris	je riais	je rie
tu ris		nous riions
il rit	FUTURE	vous riiez
nous rions	je rirai	
vous riez	PRESENT CONDITIONAL	PASSÉ SIMPLE
ils rient	je rirais	je ris

PASSÉ COMPOSÉ
j'ai ri

PAST CONDITIONAL
j'aurais ri

52.38 Savoir (*to know*)

PRESENT	IMPERFECT	PRESENT SUBJUNCTIVE
je sais	je savais	je sache
tu sais		
il sait	FUTURE	PASSÉ SIMPLE
nous savons	je saurai	je sus
vous savez	PRESENT CONDITIONAL	IMPERATIVE
ils savent	je saurais	sache

PASSÉ COMPOSÉ
j'ai su

PAST CONDITIONAL
j'aurais su

sachons
sachez

52.39 Sentir (*to feel*)

PRESENT	IMPERFECT	PRESENT SUBJUNCTIVE
je sens	je sentais	je sente
tu sens		
il sent	FUTURE	PASSÉ SIMPLE
nous sentons	je sentirai	je sentis
vous sentez	PRESENT CONDITIONAL	
ils sentent	je sentirais	

PASSÉ COMPOSÉ
j'ai senti

PAST CONDITIONAL
j'aurais senti

52.40 Servir (*to serve*)

PRESENT	IMPERFECT	PRESENT SUBJUNCTIVE
je sers	je servais	je serve
tu sers		
il sert	FUTURE	PASSÉ SIMPLE
nous servons	je servirai	je servis
vous servez		
ils servent	PRESENT CONDITIONAL	
	je servirais	
PASSÉ COMPOSÉ	PAST CONDITIONAL	
j'ai servi	j'aurais servi	

52.41 Sortir (*to go out*)

PRESENT	IMPERFECT	PRESENT SUBJUNCTIVE
je sors	je sortais	je sorte
tu sors		
il sort	FUTURE	PASSÉ SIMPLE
nous sortons	je sortirai	je sortis
vous sortez		
ils sortent	PRESENT CONDITIONAL	
	je sortirais	
PASSÉ COMPOSÉ	PAST CONDITIONAL	
je suis sorti	je serais sorti	

52.42 Suffire (*to be enough*)

PRESENT	IMPERFECT	PRESENT SUBJUNCTIVE
je suffis	je suffisais	je suffise
tu suffis		
il suffit	FUTURE	PASSÉ SIMPLE
nous suffisons	je suffirai	je suffis
vous suffisez		
ils suffisent	PRESENT CONDITIONAL	
	je suffirais	
PASSÉ COMPOSÉ	PAST CONDITIONAL	
j'ai suffi	j'aurais suffi	

52.43 Suivre (*to follow*)

PRESENT	IMPERFECT	PRESENT SUBJUNCTIVE
je suis	je suivais	je suive
tu suis		
il suit	FUTURE	PASSÉ SIMPLE
nous suivons	je suivrai	je suivis
vous suivez		
ils suivent	PRESENT CONDITIONAL	
	je suivrais	
PASSÉ COMPOSÉ	PAST CONDITIONAL	
j'ai suivi	j'aurais suivi	

52.44 Taire (*to keep quiet*)

PRESENT	IMPERFECT	PRESENT SUBJUNCTIVE
je tais	je taisais	je taise
tu tais		
il tait	FUTURE	PASSÉ SIMPLE
nous taisons	je tairai	je tus
vous taisez		
ils taisent	PRESENT CONDITIONAL	
	je tairais	
PASSÉ COMPOSÉ	PAST CONDITIONAL	
j'ai tu	j'aurais tu	

52.45 Tenir (*to hold*)

PRESENT	IMPERFECT	PRESENT SUBJUNCTIVE
je tiens	je tenais	je tienne
tu tiens		
il tient	FUTURE	PASSÉ SIMPLE
nous tenons	je tiendrai	je tins
vous tenez		tu tins
ils tiennent	PRESENT CONDITIONAL	il tint
	je tiendrais	nous tînmes
PASSÉ COMPOSÉ	PAST CONDITIONAL	vous tîntes
j'ai tenu	j'aurais tenu	ils tinrent

52.46 Vaincre (*to defeat*)

PRESENT
je vaincs
tu vaincs
il vainc
nous vainquons
vous vainquez
ils vainquent

PASSÉ COMPOSÉ
j'ai vaincu

IMPERFECT
je vainquais

FUTURE
je vaincrai

PRESENT CONDITIONAL
je vaincrais

PAST CONDITIONAL
j'aurais vaincu

PRESENT SUBJUNCTIVE
je vainque

PASSÉ SIMPLE
je vainquis

52.47 Valoir (*to be worth*)

PRESENT
je vaux
tu vaux
il vaut
nous valons
vous valez
ils valent

PASSÉ COMPOSÉ
j'ai valu

IMPERFECT
je valais

FUTURE
je vaudrai

PRESENT CONDITIONAL
je vaudrais

PAST CONDITIONAL
j'aurais valu

PRESENT SUBJUNCTIVE
je vaille

PASSÉ SIMPLE
je valus

52.48 Venir (*to come*)

PRESENT
je viens
tu viens
il vient
nous venons
vous venez
ils viennent

PASSÉ COMPOSÉ
je suis venu

IMPERFECT
je venais

FUTURE
je viendrai

PRESENT CONDITIONAL
je viendrais

PAST CONDITIONAL
je serais venu

PRESENT SUBJUNCTIVE
je vienne

PASSÉ SIMPLE
je vins
tu vins
il vint
nous vînmes
vous vîntes
ils vinrent

52.49 Vivre (*to live*)

PRESENT	IMPERFECT	PRESENT SUBJUNCTIVE
je vis	je vivais	je vive
tu vis		
il vit	FUTURE	PASSÉ SIMPLE
nous vivons	je vivrai	je vécus
vous vivez		
ils vivent	PRESENT CONDITIONAL	
	je vivrais	
PASSÉ COMPOSÉ	PAST CONDITIONAL	
j'ai vécu	j'aurais vécu	

52.50 Voir (*to see*)

PRESENT	IMPERFECT	PRESENT SUBJUNCTIVE
je vois	je voyais	je voie
tu vois		nous voyions
il voit	FUTURE	vous voyiez
nous voyons	je verrai	
vous voyez		PASSÉ SIMPLE
ils voient	PRESENT CONDITIONAL	je vis
	je verrais	
PASSÉ COMPOSÉ	PAST CONDITIONAL	
j'ai vu	j'aurais vu	

52.51 Vouloir (*to want*)

PRESENT	IMPERFECT	PRESENT SUBJUNCTIVE
je veux	je voulais	je veuille
tu veux		
il veut	FUTURE	PASSÉ SIMPLE
nous voulons	je voudrai	je voulus
vous voulez		
ils veulent	PRESENT CONDITIONAL	IMPERATIVE
	je voudrais	veuille
		veuillez
PASSÉ COMPOSÉ	PAST CONDITIONAL	
j'ai voulu	j'aurais voulu	

53 Index

This index lists key words in French and English as well as grammatical terms. Many references are included under several different headings. For example, if you want to find out how to say *his* and *her* in French, you can look up any of the following entries: *his* or *her*; **sa, son** or **ses**; "possession" or "possessive"; "adjective"; or "agreement."

A

a, an	8.1
a/à	2.1.2
à	28.1.1–28.1.2, 28.1.4, 28.2
adjectives + **à**	13.2–3
à condition de/que	49.2.1, 43.2.2
+ emphatic pronoun	17.4, 28.2.5
+ indirect object	28.2.2, 47.2
verbs + **à** + infinitive	48.2
+ **le = au**, + **les = aux**	7.1, 28.2
à mesure que	49.2.1
à moi	17.4
à moins de/que	43.2.2, 49.2.1
à peine	50.1.3
verbs + **à** + object	47.2
a lot of	28.4.3
able to	44.3
abstract nouns	7.2
accents	2
acute accent	2.1.1
cedilla	2.1.5
circumflex accent	2.1.3
diaresis	2.1.4
grave accent	2.1.2
acheter (present)	29.1
achever (present)	29.1.1
acute accent	2.1.1
active	1, 42
adjectives	11–13
+ **à**	13.2–3
agreement	11
comparative	16.1
+ conjunction	13.4
+ **de**	13.1, 13.3, 24.1.5, 27.5
de + adjective	10.2
demonstrative	18.1
endings	11
indefinite	19
irregular	11.2
plural	11
position	12
possessive	17.2

+ preposition	13.1–3
+ **que**	13.4
singular	11
superlative	16.2
adverbs	14
comparative	16.1
formation	14.1
position	15
superlative	16.2
afin de/pour	43.2.2
afin que/pour que	43.2.2, 49.2.1
age	44.6
agreement	
adjectives	11
demonstrative adjectives	18.1
indefinite adjectives	19.2.1
past participles	30.3
possessive adjectives	17.2
pronouns	22.3
ago	28.5
all	19.2.2
aller	
all tenses	52.1
present	29.3.2
to express future	35.3.2
was going to	31.2.3
alors que	49.2.1
although	49.2.1
ancien	12
another	19.2.6
any	8.2
apostrophe	3.1.1
appeler (present)	29.1.1
approximate numbers	4.1
après que	49.2.1
arriver (passé composé)	30.2
articles	7–10
definite (**le, la, l', les**)	7
indefinite (**un, une, des**)	8
indeterminate (**du, de la, de l'**)	9
no article	8.1–2
partitive (**du, de la, de l', des**)	9

use of **de**	10
as . . . (as)	16.1
asseoir s'	52.2
assez	14.2
at	28.1.4, 28.2, 28.3.1, 28.6
at about	28.1.4
au	7, 28.1.1, 28.1.3–4
au cas où	49.2.1
aucun	19.1, 19.2.7, 21.1–2
auquel	20.2.3, 27.1
aussi	26.2.1, 50.1.3
aussi (que)	16.1
aussitôt que	35.2, 49.2.1
autant (que)	16.1
autre	19.2.6–7
aux	7, 28.1.1
auxiliary verbs	1
auxquel(le)s	20.2.3, 27.1, 27.4
avant de	43.2.2
avant que	21.5, 43.2.2, 49.2.1
avoir	
present	29.3.2
all tenses	52.3
passé composé with **avoir**	30.1
special uses	44.6
ayant	40.1

B
bad	14.2
badly	14.2
battre	52.4
beaucoup de	28.4.3
because	49.2.1
before	43.2.2
best	16.2
better	16.1
bien	14.2
with conditional	38.2
bien que	49.2.1
bientôt	14.2
bigger, biggest	16
boire	52.5
bon, bonne	11.2, 14.2
by	28.1.2, 42.2

C
c'	3.1.1
ça	18.2.3
can	44.3
capital letters	3.2
car	49.1
cardinal numbers	4.1

cedilla	2.1.5
ce	
adjective	18.1
ce...-ci/-là	18.1
ce ne sont pas des...	10.1
ce n'est pas un...	10.1
ce sont	8.2, 26.2.1
pronoun	18.2.2
qui/que	27.3
ceci	18.2.3
cela	18.2.3
celle	18.2.1
celle-ci, celle-là	18.2.1
celles	18.2.1
celui	18.2.1
celui-ci, celui-là	18.2.1
cent	4.1, 8.1
c'est	8.1, 26.2.1
certain	19.1, 19.2.7
ces	18.1
cet, cette	18.1
ceux	18.2.1
ceux-ci, ceux-là	18.2.1
chacun	19.1
chaque	19.1
chez	28.6
-ci	18.1
circumflex accent	2.1.3
clause	1
color	11.1
comma	3.1.3
commands	41
comme	20.4, 49.2.1
comment (question word)	20.2.5
comparative	16.1
see also superlative	16.2
comparison	16
compound nouns	6.2
compound tenses	30, 32, 34, 36, 38, 43.3.1., 43.3.3
future perfect tense	36
passé composé	30
past conditional tense	38
past subjunctive tense	43.3.1
pluperfect subjunctive tense	43.3.3
pluperfect tense	32
preterite perfect	34
conditional present	37
conditional past	38
conduire (present)	29.3.1, 52.6

conjunctions	49
coordinating	49.1
subordinating	49.2
conjugation	51
connaître	44.4, 52.7
coordinating conjunctions	49.1
continuous tenses	29.4.1, 31.2.3, 40.1.3
coudre	52.8
could	37.2, 44.3
could have	38.2
countries	
use of articles	7.2
with **en, au, aux**	28.1.1
courir	52.9
craindre	52.10
croire	52.11
cueillir	52.12
cuire	52.13

D

d'	3.1.1
d'autres	19.2.7
dans	28.1.1, 28.1.4
date	28.1.4
davantage	16.1
days, preceded by **le**	7.2
de	
adjectives taking **de**	13.1
article	8.1–2, 10
de... à	28.1.4
de crainte que	21.5
de façon que	49.2.1
de l', de la	9
de + le = du	7.1
de + les = des	7.1
de manière que	49.2.1
de même que	49.2.1
de peur que	21.5, 49.2.1
de sorte que	49.2.1
possession	17.1
preposition	16.2, 17.1, 28.1.4, 28.4
verbs followed by **de**	47.3, 48.3
decimals	3.1.3
definite articles	7
demonstratives	18
adjectives	18.1
pronouns	18.2
depuis	28.5
+ imperfect	31.2
depuis que	49.2.1
dernier + subjunctive	43.2.3

des	
after **ce sont**	8.1
= **de + les**	7.1
some	8.2
dès que	35.2, 49.2.1
desquel(le)s	27.1
devenir (passé composé)	30.2
devoir	
all tenses	52.14
present	29.3.2
use	44.1
diaresis	2.1.4
dire	
all tenses	52.15
on dirait que	46.4.2
present	29.3.2
direct object	1
verb + direct object	47.1
direct object pronouns	23.1–2
direct question	20.1
disjunctive pronouns	26.2, 28.2.5
distance	28.2.1
donc	49.1
dont	27.5
dormir	52.16
du/dû	2.1.3
du article	9
du... au	28.1.4
du/des	7.1
from	28.1.4
due to	44.1
duquel	27.1

E

é	2.1.1, 2.1.2
è	2.1.2
each	19.1
écrire	52.17
elle(s)	
emphatic pronoun	26.2
subject pronoun	22
emphatic pronouns	26.2, 28.2.5
en	
en attendant que	49.2.1
en train de	29.4.1
pronoun	24
preposition	28.1.1–4, 28.3
+ present participle	40.1.2
with indefinite pronouns	19.2.7
endings	
adjectives	11
-ing	40.1

■ **Index**

verbs	51.1
enough	14.2
entre + lequel	27.4.1
entrer (passé composé)	30.2
envoyer	52.18
épeler (present)	29.1
espérer (present)	29.1
est-ce que	20.1
et	49.1
être	
all tenses	52.19
forming **passé composé**	30.2
forming passive	42.1
present	29.3.2
use	44
eux	26.2
every	19.2.2
everything	19.2.2
exclamations	20.4

F

faire	
all tenses	52.20
(present)	29.3.2
falloir	52.21
il faut (use)	44.5
feminine	
adjectives	11
nouns	5
finir (present)	29.2
for	
for fear that	21.5
time	28.5
from	28.4.1
future	35
use of present tense	29.4.2
use of **aller**	35.3
future perfect	36

G

geler (present)	29.1
gender	1
geographical names	7.2
with prepositions	28.1.1
good	11.2, 14.2
going to	29.4.2, 31.2.3
grave accent	2.1.4
guère	21.1–2

H

haïr	52.22
have to	44.1
he	22

her	
object pronoun	23.1
possessive adjective	17.2
hers	17.3
him	23.1
his	
possessive adjective	17.2
hyphen	3.1.2
silent **h**	3.1.1

I

I	32
if	49.2.1
no future tense	29.4.2
no conditional tense	37.2
il(s)	22
il est + adjective + que	13.4
il existe	46.2.2
il fait (beau, etc.)	46.1
il faut	44.5
il paraît que	46.4.1
il pleut	46, 52.32
il reste	46.2.3
il s'agit de	46.6.1
il se peut que	46.6.3
il se trouve que	46.6.2
il semble que	46.4.2
il suffit	46.5
il vaut mieux	46.3
il + verb	46
il y a	
ago	28.5
there is/are	46.2.1
imperative	41
imperfect	31
imperfect or **passé composé**	31.3
imperfect subjunctive	43.3.2
impersonal verbs	46
in 28.1.1, 28.1.3–4, 28.3, 28.4.4, 28.4.6	
indefinite adjectives	19
indefinite	
articles	8
pronouns	19
indefinites + subjunctive	43.2.5
indeterminates (**du, de la, de l', de**)	9
indicative	43.1.1
indirect	
object pronouns	23.1–2
questions	20.3
verbs taking indirect objects	47
infinitive	39

past infinitive	39.1.2
preceded by **à**	48.2
preceded by **de**	48.3
preceded by **ne pas**	39.1.3
preceded by verb	48.1
-ing ending	40.1
inversion	20.1, 50.1
interrogative	
adjectives	20.2.2
pronouns	20.2
irregular adverbs	14
irregular comparatives	16.1
irregular verbs	29.3
verb tables	52
it	22.3
it is	8.1, 10.1, 26.2.1

J

j'	22.1
jamais	21.1–2
je	22
jeter (present)	29.1.1
jusqu'à	28.1.4
jusqu'à ce que	49.2
jusqu'au	28.1.4
just	29.4.4, 31.2

K

know	44.3–4

L

l'	
article	7
object pronoun	23.1
la	
article	7
object pronoun	23.1
la/là	2.1.2
-là	18.1
languages	7.2
laquelle	
question word	20.2.3
relative pronoun	27.1, 27.4
le	
article	7
le mien	17.3
le leur	17.3
le moins que/de	16.2
le nôtre	17.3
le plus que/de	16.2
le tien	17.3
le vôtre	17.3
object pronoun	23.1

least	16.1
lequel	
question word	20.2.3
relative pronoun	27.1, 27.4
les	
article	7
object pronoun	23.1
lesquel(le)s	
question word	20.2.3
relative pronoun	27.1, 27.4
less (than)	16.1
leur(s) adjective	17.2
leur	
object pronoun	23.1
leur, le/la	17.3
leurs, les	17.3
lever (present)	29.1.1
libérer (present)	29.1.1
linking words	49
lire	52.23
loin	14.2
lorsque	49.2.1
with future	35.2
lots	28.4.3
lui	
emphatic pronoun	26.2
object pronoun	23.1

M

m'	23.1
ma	17.2
mais	49.1
mal	14.2
malgré que	49.2.1
many	28.4.3
masculine	
nouns	5
adjectives	11
mauvais	12, 14.2
may	44.3
me	
object pronoun	23.1
reflexive pronoun	26.1
measurement	28.4.5
meilleur	14.2, 16.1
même	12, 19.2.3, 26.2.1
mes	17.2
mettre	53.24
mien, le; mienne, la	17.3
mieux	14.2, 16.1
might	37.2
mille	4.1

mine	17.3
modal verbs	44
moi	23.1, 26.2
moindre	16.1
moins,	
le	16.2
moins que/de	16.1
mon	17.2
monter (passé composé)	30.2
mood	1
more (than)	16.1
most	16.2
mourir	52.25
passé composé with **être**	30.2
much	28.4.3
my	17.2

N

n'	3.1.1
nager (present)	29.1.3
naître	52.26
nationality	8.2
ne (see also negatives)	21, 21.5
leaving out **ne**	21.3
ne... aucun	21.1
ne... guère	21.1
ne... jamais	21.1
ne... ni... ni	21.1
ne... nulle part	21.1
ne... pas	21.1
ne... pas + infinitive	39.1.3
ne... personne	21.1
ne... plus	21.1
ne... que	10.1, 21.1
ne... rien	21.1
negatives (see also **ne**)	21
commands	41.2.2
leaving out part of negation	21.3–4
position	21.2
use of **de** with negations	10.1
with infinitive	39.1.3
neither	21.1
never	21.1
ni... ni	21.1
nobody/no one	21.1
non plus	21.1, 21.3
nos	17.2
not	21.1
nothing	21.1
notre	17.2
nôtre, le/la; nôtres, les	17.3
noun phrases	50.3.5

nouns	5
gender	5
noun phrases	50.3.5
plural of nouns	6
nous	
emphatic pronoun	26.2
object pronoun	23.1
reflexive pronoun	26.1
subject pronoun	22
numbers	4
approximate	4.1
cardinal	4.1
le + number	7.2
ordinal	4.2

O

object pronouns	23
direct or indirect?	23.2
position	23.3, 41.2
verbs used with	47
occupations	8.1
of	28.4.2
of which, of whom	27.5
offrir (present)	29.2
on	22.4, 28.2.1, 28.7, 42.2
on dirait que	46.4.2
on	28.2.1, 28.7
one	
number	4.1
pronoun	22
only	21.1
or	49.1
or	49.1
order of object pronouns	23.3
ordinal numbers	4.2
other	19.2.6
ou	49.1
ou/où	2.1.2
où	
relative pronoun	27.6
question word	20.1
ought to	44.1
ouvrir	
all tenses	52.27
present	29.2
our	17.2
ours	17.3

P

par	28.1.4
commencer par	48.4
finir par	48.4

with a passive	42.1
paraître	52.28
parce que	49.2.1
parler (present)	29.1
parmi + **lequel**	27.4.1
participles	40
agreement rules	30.3
past participle	40.2
present participle	40.1
partir	52.29
partitive articles	9
parts of the body	7.2
pas	21.1–2
leaving out **pas**	21.4
passé composé tense	30
with **avoir**	30.1
with **être**	30.2
use	30.4
passé simple tense	33
passive	42
past conditional tense	38
past infinitive	39.1.2
past participle	40.2
agreement	30.3
past subjunctive	43.3.1
payer (present)	29.1.2
peindre	52.30
pendant	28.5
pendant que	49.2.1
+ future	35.2
per	28.2.1
perfect tense *see* **passé composé** tense	
personal pronouns	22
personne (ne)	21.1–2
with **de** + adjective	19.2.8
+ subjunctive	43.2.3
peser (present)	29.1.1
peut-être	50.1.3
pire	16.1
plaire	
all tenses	52.31
present	29.3.1
pleuvoir	52.32
pluperfect tense	32
pluperfect subjunctive	43.3.3
plural	
adjectives	11
nouns	6
plus	
comparative	16.1
negative	21.1–3

superlative	16.2
plusieurs	19.1, 19.2.7–8
position of	
adjectives	12
adverbs	15
personal pronouns	23.3
possession	17, 28.2.5
with **de**	17.1
possessives	17
adjectives	17.2
pronouns	17.3
pour + infinitive	43.2.2
pour que	43.2.2, 49.2.1
pourvu que	49.2.1
pouvoir	
all tenses	52.33
present	29.3.2
use	44.3
préférer (present)	29.1
premier/première	4.2
+ subjunctive	43.2.3
prendre	
all tenses	52.34
present	29.3.1
prepositions	28
à	28.2
chez	28.6
de	28.4
depuis	28.5
en	28.3
il y a	28.5
of time	28.1.4
pendant	28.5
sur	28.7
with geographical names	28.1.1
with means of transport	28.1.2
with months, seasons, and years	
	28.1.3
present	29
present continuous tense	29.4.1
use	29.4
present conditional tense	37
present participle	40.1
present subjunctive	43.1–2
preterite perfect tense	34
prices	
+ **de**	28.4.5
+ **le**	7.2
with **à**	28.2.3
profession	8.1–2
pronouns	22–27

after prepositions 26.2.1
direct object 23.1–2
demonstrative 18.2
disjunctive 26.2
emphatic 26.2
en 24
indefinite 19
indirect object 23.1–2
object 23
position of 23.3
possessive 17.3
reflexive 26.1
relative 27
subject 22
y 25
proper nouns (plural) 6.3
propre 12
punctuation 3.1
puisque 49.2.1

Q
qu' 3.1.1
quand 49.2.1
+ future 29.4.2
qu'est-ce que/qui 20.2.1
que
adjective + **que** 13.4
conjunction 49.2.1
in exclamations 20.4
que, ne 21.1–2
question word 20.2.1
relative pronoun 27.1–3
quel(s)
in exclamations 20.4
question word 20.2.2
quelle(s)
in exclamations 20.4
question word 20.2.2
quelque 19.2.5
quelque chose de +
adjective 19.2.8
quelqu'un 19.2.8
quelques-uns 19.2.7
quelqu'un de + adjective 19.2.8
quelqu'un qui/que +
subjunctive 43.2.3
questions 20
comment 20.2.5
direct 20.1
est-ce que 20.1
indirect 20.3
inversion 20.1

lequel 20.2.3
quel 20.2.2
question words 20.2
question words with
prepositions 20.2.4
quoi 20.2.5
qui
question word 20.2.1
relative pronoun 27.1–4
qui est-ce que/qui 20.2.1
quoi
question word 20.2.4–5
relative pronoun 27.4
quoique 49.2.1
quotation marks 3.1.4

R
recevoir 52.35
reflexive pronouns 45
reflexive verbs 45
agreement rules 30.3.2
impersonal forms 46.6
perfect with **être** 30.2
regular verb endings 51.1
relative pronouns 27
with emphatic pronouns 26.2.1
renouveler (present) 29.1
rentrer (passé composé) 30.2
résoudre 52.36
rester (passé composé) 30.2
rien, de 19.2.8
rien, ne 21.1.2
rien + subjunctive 43.2.3
rire 52.37

S
s' 3.1.1
sa 17.2
same 19.1
sans + infinitive 43.2.2
sans que 49.2.1
savoir
all tenses 52.38
present 29.3.2
use 44.3.2
vs **connaître** 44.4
se 26.1
seasons
use of **le** 7.2
with prepositions 28.1.3
self 19.2.3, 26.2.1
sentence 1

sentir	
all tenses	52.39
servir	52.40
seul	12
+ subjunctive	43.2.3
with emphatic pronoun	26.2.1
ses	17.2
several	19.1
she	22
should	37.2, 44.1
should have	38.2
si	49.2.1
+ imperfect tense	37.2
+ present tense	29.4.2
sien, le; sienne, la; sien(ne)s, les	17.3
silent **h**	3.1.1
simple	12
simple tenses	1
future tense	35
imperfect tense	31
imperfect subjunctive tense	43.3.2
passé simple tense	33
present conditional tense	37
present subjunctive tense	43.1
present tense	29
since	28.5
singular	
adjectives	11
nouns	5
soi	26.3
soon	14.2
some	8.2, 9, 19.2.5
son	17.2
sortir	
all tenses	52.41
passé composé	30.2
souffrir (present—for full	
conjugation *see* **ouvrir**)	29.2
speech marks	3.1.4
speed	
use of **le**	7.2
with **à**	28.2.1
sports—use of **le**	7.2
stem	51.2
subject	1
subject pronouns	22
subjunctive	43
imperfect tense	43.3.2
past tense	43.3.1
pluperfect tense	43.3.3
present tense	43.1

use	43.2
subordinating conjunctions	49.2
such	19.2.4
suffire	52.42
suivre	52.43
superlative	16.2, 28.4.4
see also comparative	16.1
+ subjunctive	43.2.3
supposed to	44.1
sur	28.7
T	
-t- (in a question)	20.1
t'	23.1
ta	17.2
taire	52.44
tandis que	49.2.1
tant que + future	35.2
te	23.1
reflexive pronoun	26.1
tel	19.2.4
tellement que	49.2.1
tenir	
all tenses	52.45
present	29.2
tenses	29–40
future	35
future perfect	36
imperfect	31
passé composé	30
passé simple	33
past conditional	38
present	29
present conditional	37
preterite perfect	34
pluperfect	32
subjunctive	
imperfect	43.3.2
past	43.3.1
pluperfect	43.3.3
present	43.1
tes	17.2
than	16.1, 28.4.4
that	27.1, 49.2.1
the	7
their, theirs	17.2–3
them	23.1
there is/are/was, etc.	46.2
these	18
they	22
this	18
those	18

thousands	3.1.3
tien, le; tienne, la; tien(ne)s, les	17.3
titles—use of **le, la**	7.2
time (prepositions)	28.1.4
to	28.1.1, 28.2
to be	
all tenses	52.19
present	29.3.2
translations	44.6
to be able to	44.3
to be due to	44.1
to be going to	29.4.2, 31.2.3
to be supposed to	44.1
to be used to	31.2.2
to him/her	23.1
to them	23.1
toi	23.1, 26.2
tomber (passé composé)	30.2
ton	17.2
tout (e, es), tous	
adjective	19.2.2
en + present participle	40.1.2
pronoun	19.2.2
transport	28.1.2
tu	22
tu/vous	22.2
turn, my	17.4, 28.2.5
U	
un/une	
number	4.1
article	8
unless	21.5
until	28.1.4, 49.2.1
us	23.1
used to	31.2.2
V	
vaincre	52.46
valoir	52.47
valoir mieux	46.3
venir	
all tenses	52.48
passé composé	30.2
present	29.2
venir de	29.4.4
in the imperfect	31.2.3
verb conjugation	
verbs in **-aire**	29.3.1
verbs in **-aître**	29.3.1
verbs in **-ayer**	29.1.2
verbs in **-cer**	29.1.3
verbs in **-e/é** + consonant +	
er	29.1.1
verbs in **-er**	29.1
verbs in **-ger**	29.1.3
verbs in **-indre**	29.3.1
verbs in **-ir**	29.2
verbs in **-oir**	29.3
verbs in **-re**	29.3
verbs in **-yer**	29.1.2
verb tables	52
verb constructions	
+ **à** + infinitive	48.2
+ **à** + object	47.2
+ **de** + infinitive	48.3
+ **de** + object	47.3
+ direct object	47.1
+ indirect object	47.2
+ infinitive	48.1
verbs *see* compound tenses	
commands	41
conditional tenses	37–38
continuous tenses	29.4.1, 31.2.3,
	40.1.3
endings	51.1
future tense	35
future perfect tense	36
imperfect tense	31
imperative	41
impersonal verbs	46
indicative	1, 42.3.1
infinitive	39
-ing form	40.1
irregular verbs	29.3, 52
modal verbs	44
participles	40
past	40.2
present	40.1
passé composé tense	30
passé simple tense	33
passive	42
past conditional tense	38
past participle	40.2
present conditional tense	37
present participle	40.1
present tense	29
preterite perfect tense	34
pluperfect tense	32
reflexive verbs	45
stem	51.2
subjunctive	43
imperfect tense	43.3.2

passé composé tense	43.3.1
pluperfect tense	43.3.3
present tense	43.1
use	43.2
verb tables	52
vers	28.1.4
vivre	52.49
voir	52.50
vos	17.2
votre	17.2
vôtre, le/la	17.3
vôtres, les	17.3
vouloir	
all tenses	52.51
present	29.3.2
use	44.2
vous	
as opposed to **tu**	22.2
emphatic pronoun	26.2
object pronoun	23.1
reflexive pronoun	26.1
subject pronoun	22

W

we	22
weather	46.1
in the past	31.3
well	14.2
what	20.2.1, 27.3
when	49.2.1

where	27.6, 49.2
which	
of which	27.5
question word	20.2.2
relative pronoun	27.4.2
while	49.2.1
who	
question word	20.2.1
relative pronoun	27.1–2
whom	
of whom	27.5
question word	20.2.1
relative pronoun	27.1–2
whose	27.5
with (staying with someone)	28.6
word order	50
worse	16.1
worst	16.2
would	37.2
would you . . .	41.1
would have	38.2

Y

you	
emphatic pronoun	26.2
object pronoun	23.2
subject pronoun	22
your	17.2
yours	17.3